Rangeand
Endurance

Range and Endurance

Frank Hitchens

The Crowood Press

First published in 2007 by
Airlife Publishing, an imprint of
The Crowood Press Ltd
Ramsbury, Marlborough
Wiltshire SN8 2HR

www.crowood.com

British Library Cataloguing-in-Publication Data
A catalogue record for this book is available from the British Library.

ISBN 978 1 86126 920 1

Edited and designed by Ian Penberthy

Printed and bound in Spain by Graphy Cems

CONTENTS

INTRODUCTION

On 14 December 1986, Dick Rutan and Jeanne Yeager left Edwards Air Force base, in California, in their purpose-built aircraft, *Voyager*, on the first around-the-world, non-stop, unrefuelled flight. They covered a total distance of 25,012 statute miles in 216 hours, 3 minutes and 44 seconds – truly a flight of great range and endurance. Their names and achievement will stand forever in the annals of aviation history, alongside those of John Alcock and Arthur Brown, Charles Lindbergh, Wiley Post and many others.

For the average light aircraft pilot, flights of up to 350 nautical miles or about three hours duration are more the norm. Nevertheless, flying for range and endurance is no less important. In these days of ever rising fuel prices, getting the best range per gallon requires flying the aircraft as efficiently as possible with regard to wind velocity, altitude, power settings, aircraft weight and choice of route. Fuel management before and during flight, and making precise calculations of fuel consumption are just as important. To this end, a complete knowledge of the aircraft's fuel system and correct leaning schedule is essential to achieve safe, fuel-efficient flight.

Mismanagement of any part of the fuel system can, and does, lead to unnecessary emergencies. Every year, aircraft are landed short of their destinations due to fuel mismanagement problems. Some experience in-flight engine failures during the cruise, leading to forced landings. In such situations, many pilots achieve safe landings, while others damage the aircraft and cause injury, or even death, to the aircraft's occupants. Subsequently, some of these aircraft are discovered to be completely out of fuel, while others still have sufficient fuel in another tank that would have allowed a safe continuation to the destination. Any small error or omission when handling the fuel system can result in an engine failure, which, if not corrected quickly, can result in a forced landing. This can happen to any of us, at any time. In the USA, statistics indicate that 9–12 per cent of all accidents are related to fuel mismanagement problems. Over half of these accidents are caused by fuel exhaustion due to faulty flight planning and/or handling of the fuel system. This means that fuel mismanagement accidents are on a par with those caused by stalls, during take-off, climb and descent, and by mechanical problems. It only takes a small amount of common sense to avoid a fuel problem. My hope is that this book will make you aware of the pitfalls and help prevent you from becoming a statistic due to fuel mismanagement.

I speak from experience, as I have been responsible for a fuel mismanagement problem while flying a single-engine aircraft. It occurred at an airport with an over-water approach path. My fellow pilot, who was flying the approach, was not too familiar with the type of aircraft or with the airport where we were about to land. I suggested that he slow down to approach speed to allow a departing aircraft time to get airborne. The engine rpm reduced as he throttled back, and then he announced that we were losing power. There was no response from the engine as he pushed the throttle fully forward. My first real engine failure! We were still over water at 1,000ft with about two miles to run to reach the airport; no chance of a 'dead stick' landing there. Half-way through the engine failure check-list, to our surprise, the engine suddenly burst back into life at full power, the throttle being still fully forward. We continued on to make a normal landing on the runway. Fuel mismanagement was the cause of the problem. Instead of applying carburettor heat before reducing power, the pilot had pulled the mixture control to 'idle cut-off', starving the engine of fuel!

It is not only pilots of light aircraft who experience fuel related problems; professional pilots are also guilty of causing them! The crew of one airliner inadvertently turned off the fuel to both engines just after take-off. Luckily, they discovered their error before it was too late. An Air Canada Boeing 767, on a flight from Montreal to Edmonton, landed short of its destination on a small airstrip at Gimla, Manitoba. Faulty fuel gauges and an error in converting between litres and US gallons by both refuellers and flight crew had resulted in only half the required fuel being loaded on board the aircraft before flight! Fortunately, the powerless landing at Gimla resulted in only minor airframe damage and no injury to the occupants. In 1980, a Vickers Viscount landed in a paddock in Devon following fuel starvation, which resulted in a few injuries. Other airline crews have experienced similar problems with less favourable results.

Flying for range and endurance is not simply a matter of 'going the distance' or using the aircraft and fuel efficiently; it also involves the correct and common-sense handling of the fuel system. Mismanaging the fuel system, as the incidents described previously show, can quickly terminate the flight well short of its true range and endurance.

I have written this book mainly with the private pilot and new commercial pilot in mind, flying light single- and twin-engined aircraft. Pilots with greater experience may also benefit from reading it, however, using it as a refresher on range and endurance flying. It starts with a brief look at fuel technology, followed by a consideration of different fuel leaning procedures. Next, aircraft fuel systems are covered, followed by the practical aspects and theory of fuel management. Then comes the all-important aspect of pre-flight planning, after which range and endurance are discussed from an aerodynamic point of view. Finally, it concludes with a selection of formulas for solving fuel calculation problems on the E6-B air navigation computer.

As the pilot in command, you should be familiar with, and use, the flight manual or pilot's operating handbook (POH) for the aircraft you fly. This point cannot be overemphasized, as the flight manual is the number-one publication for your aircraft and its systems. Once you have an understanding of the manual and the operation of your aircraft's fuel system, and have read this book, you should be able to conduct every flight professionally with regard to flying for range and endurance. An important aspect of good airmanship is being able to conduct each flight to its safe termination, using fuel economically and arriving with sufficient reserve in the tanks. I hope that this book will help you to achieve the objective of safe and fuel efficient flight.

In conclusion, I would like to thank my good friend Nathan Bullmore for his assistance in scanning the diagrams and photographs for this book. Also, I would like to thank Wellington Aero Club instructor Nicolla Wall for the assistance she gave me when I photographed the club's Piper Tomahawk being refuelled. Their help is greatly appreciated. All the photographs in this book are from the my own collection.

Fly safely with knowledge.

Frank Hitchens
Wellington, New Zealand
2007

CHAPTER 1
FUEL TECHNOLOGY

One of the biggest expenses of operating an aircraft, whether a light single or a heavy jet transport, is the cost of fuel. Running an aircraft economically and getting the most range from a given quantity of fuel requires an excellent knowledge of the aircraft's fuel system, leaning techniques and fuel management, both before and in flight. It also helps to have a general appreciation of the fuel's limitations and abilities. Therefore, I'll begin this study of flying for range and endurance with a brief look at fuel technology.

Crude petroleum oil is one of the world's natural resources, having been formed many millions of years ago from decaying plant and animal matter. It was eventually discovered by geologists deep beneath the earth's surface in various parts of the world. The location of an oil field determines the crude oil's chemical composition, its physical properties and its quality, which can vary from place to place. The oil refining industry had its beginnings when James Williams opened the world's first oil refinery in Canada in 1857. In 1859, at Titusville, Pennsylvania, E.l. Drake drilled the first well specifically for the purpose of obtaining oil. Samuel Van Sickyl further developed the multi-step refining process, in common use today, in 1877 in the USA.

The process of refining crude oil into petroleum is complex, and a complete explanation is beyond the scope of this book. However, it is worth having a brief look at the basic steps before studying the fuel's different characteristics.

Crude oil passes through three basic refining processes to become its finished products. In the first process of distillation, it is heated in a 'still'. As the temperature of the crude oil rises, petrol (or Avgas) boils off at around 200°C (392°F). This is followed by kerosene, diesel oil and turbine fuel, which evaporates at 180–345°C (356–653°F). Other by-products, known collectively as 'fractions', vaporize at different temperatures. The fractions are allowed to cool and condense into liquids, or distillates, for further refining. The lighter elements (iso-butane is the lightest) boil off at lower temperatures, while the heavier elements (naphthalene is the heaviest) become gases at higher temperatures. Treating and blending are also parts of the first stage, which isolates the various products. The second stage of the refining process is known as 'cracking'. This causes the various chemical compounds to condense. The third process involves 'reforming', or producing the final products.

Petroleum oil consists of 50–98 per cent hydrocarbons, the remaining

For airlines and private operators, however, the fuel bill is one of the biggest expenses in operating their aircraft. The lower the fuel price, the greater the profit margin.

So, why does JP-5 cost more than Jet A-1? The reason is quite simple: for each barrel of crude oil, 23 per cent is used to produce JP-5 fuel, whereas only 11.5 per cent is needed to make Jet A-1.

Jet A-1 is also slightly lighter in weight than JP-5, which is another advantage for the civil operator. Carrying less weight in fuel allows more weight to be carried in revenue earning passengers and freight. And that's what flying for range is all about – using fuel efficiently.

Avgas, with a lower flash point than any jet fuel, could be considered a disadvantage. However, the volume of fuel carried by a piston-engine aircraft is very small compared to the amount carried by a jet transport.

SPECIFIC GRAVITY

The density of a substance is defined as mass per unit volume, measured in kilograms per cubic metre or pounds per cubic feet. It involves the relationship between the mass of the substance and its temperature. By comparing the density of a given mass with an equal mass of water at a temperature of 4°C (39°F), the specific gravity (sp. gr.) or relative density of the substance (fuel) can be found. Specific gravity is a ratio and is expressed as a fraction:

$$\text{Specific gravity} = \frac{\text{Mass of substance (fuel)}}{\text{Mass of equal volume of water at } 4°C \ (39°C)}$$

Because the density of water varies and attains its maximum value of approximately 1,000kg/cu.m (62.5lb/cu.ft) at 4°C (39°F), this figure is used for the basis of calculations. At either side of 4°C (39°F), the density of water will decrease, while its volume will expand. The density of solids does not vary by a great amount, unlike the density of liquids and gases, which vary with temperature and pressure. (Remember Charles' and Boyle's laws concerning the temperature, volume and pressure of gasses.) Liquids such as methylated spirit and turpentine have a density greater than water, but aviation fuel and most other fluids have a lower density, which is why their relative density is referred to that of water. A fuel's specific gravity will vary with temperature, density and octane rating. The density, specific gravity and mass of fuel will all decrease with a rise in temperature, but there will be a increase in volume. Conversely, the density, specific gravity and mass will increase with a drop in temperature down to -15°C (5°F), at which point it remains constant.

The graph in Figure 1 shows that density decreases (as does specific gravity by a smaller amount) with a rise in fuel temperature, while the volume increases. Also, water achieves its maximum density at 4°C (39°F) and the fuel's maximum density is found at -15°C (5°F). We can find the mass of a

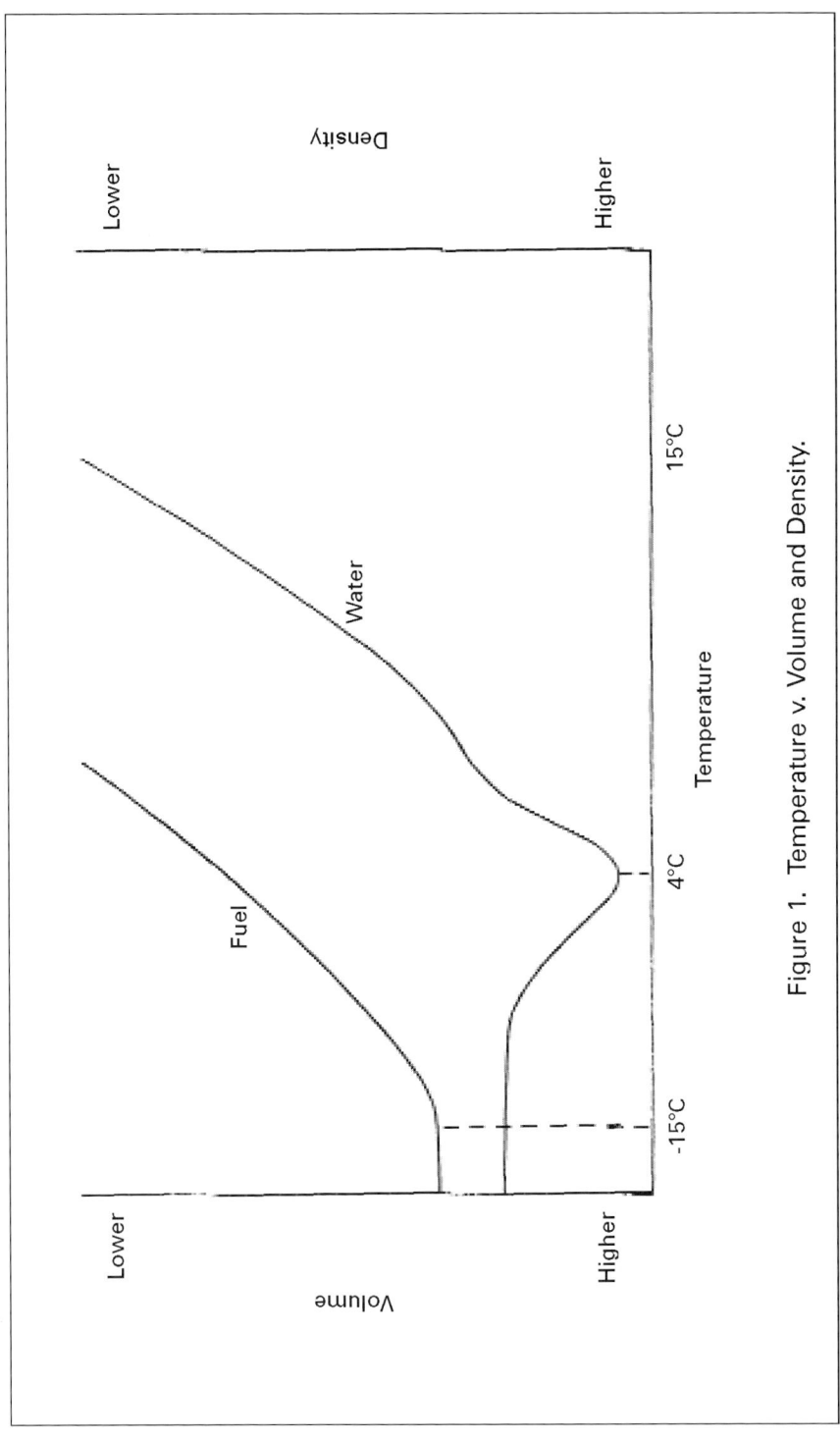

Figure 1. Temperature v. Volume and Density.

The Cessna 207 is the largest piston-engine single built by Cessna, being eclipsed only by the turbo-prop Cessna Caravan. It can carry up to seven passengers over a distance of 480–810n.miles (550–930st.miles), depending on altitude, power setting and whether standard or long-range fuel tanks are fitted. Its 300bhp Continental IO-520-F engine uses 100/130-octane fuel.

given volume of fuel by multiplying that volume in litres (or gallons) by the given specific gravity for that fuel. This can easily be done on the E6-B air navigation computer (*see* Fuel Calculation Formulas). Although density and specific gravity go hand in hand, the difference between their definitions should be appreciated:

- Density is mass per unit volume.
- Specific gravity is the ratio of the density of the substance (fuel) to the density of water at 4°C (39°F).

For pilots of light aircraft, the change in fuel density with temperature is of little consequence because their aircraft carry a relatively small amount of fuel. It is of greater significance for pilots of large transport aircraft, however, who must carry out fuel calculations prior to flight. It is important to remember that the fuel's volume will increase with a rise in temperature. If tanks are topped off with cold fuel early in the day, the fuel may expand and overflow later if it warms up because the aircraft has been left standing out in the sun.

Different types of fuel have different energy content, specified as the number of joules per kilogram. A fuel with a lower specific gravity (relative density) will have a greater energy content per kilogram than one of higher specific gravity. Jet fuel, for example, at 6.7lb/USgal is denser than Avgas at 6.0lb/USgal. Consequently, there is a greater change in its density with temperature than occurs with Avgas. For this reason, fuel requirements for large aircraft are measured in mass rather than volume, hence the need to convert between gallons and pounds.

DETONATION AND PRE-IGNITION

One of the most important characteristics of a piston engine's fuel is its resistance to 'knock' or detonation. High-octane fuels have a better resistance to knock, which is of greater importance in high-power engines. A jet engine burns fuel at a constant pressure and does not have to contend with the changing pressure caused by the Otto cycle in a piston engine. Therefore, knock is of no importance to a jet engine, but specific gravity and calorific value are relevant.

Increasing the pressure of the fuel/air mixture in the cylinders will raise the temperature of the burning mixture. This, in turn, will increase the engine's brake horsepower and thermal efficiency. That said, if the pressure is raised too high, detonation will occur and increase the compression in the cylinders even further, in some cases up to around 281kg/sq.cm (4,000lb/sq.in). This is considerably more than the normal operating pressure of 28–35kg/sq.cm (400–500lb/sq.in). With the increased cylinder pressure occurring closer to top dead centre on the piston's travel, greater stress will be placed on the pistons, cylinder walls, crankshaft and bearings, possibly leading to fractures and subsequent engine failure. Detonation can also be instigated by hot spots within the cylinders; poor-quality fuel; the wrong mixture setting for the altitude and power setting; and using fuel with an octane rating that is too low for the power of the engine. High-octane fuel has the benefit of a longer self-ignition delay compared to low-octane fuel, thereby decreasing the likelihood of detonation.

Under normal operating conditions, the flame front will spread across the combustion chamber from the spark plugs, burning the mixture at a steady rate of 21–30m/sec. (70–100ft/sec.). The fuel/air ratio, temperature and type of fuel determine the actual speed of the flame front. When detonation occurs, the fuel/air mixture is ignited almost instantaneously, causing an explosive and sudden increase of pressure in the cylinders. This pressure is transmitted down to the connecting rods and crankshaft bearings. With cylinder-head temperatures reaching melting point, the engine can suffer severe structural damage. If you suspect detonation in flight, reduce power to a lower setting. In a car, it is heard as a 'pinking' sound, but in a light aircraft there is too much engine and slipstream noise for the pilot to be able to hear it. Correct engine management is essential to prevent detonation.

Pre-ignition is similar to detonation, but whereas detonation occurs after the spark plug has fired, pre-ignition takes place before a spark is produced.

In this case, the fuel/air mixture is ignited by overheated spark plugs or exhaust valves, or incandescent carbon deposits in the cylinders. The results of pre-ignition are:

- Rough engine running.
- A reduction in engine power.
- A rise in cylinder-head temperature.
- Engine backfiring.
- Damage to valves, spark plugs, pistons and cylinder heads.

Detonation can be caused if the symptoms of pre-ignition persist.

It can be rather difficult to distinguish the difference between detonation and pre-ignition in flight, because both could be occurring at the same time. In addition, detonation could occur in any number of cylinders, whereas pre-ignition is usually confined to one or maybe two cylinders. The common type of cylinder-head temperature (CHT) gauge, which has a thermocouple attached to only one cylinder, will not detect pre-ignition or detonation if either condition takes place in any of the other cylinders. An electronic gauge with a thermocouple attached to each cylinder will quickly indicate the rise in temperature in the relevant cylinder. To prevent running on when stopping an engine (due to pre-ignition), the idle cut-off is used to shut off the fuel supply to the engine before turning off the ignition. This way, a smooth shutdown is achieved without placing undue stress on the engine.

OCTANE RATING

When processing crude oil to produce fuel, a refinery's chemists ensure that the fuel conforms to certain specifications. Anti-detonation (or anti-knock) characteristic is one such major specification. A measure of this characteristic is the octane number, (or anti-knock rating), introduced by Graham Edgar of the Ethyl Gasoline Company, in the USA during the late 1920s. This was extended to include the double-figure performance numbers around 1939.

The octane rating is found by comparing the detonation characteristics of a given fuel with the characteristics of a known percentage of iso-octane in a blend of iso-octane and heptane. Iso-octane is a hydrocarbon from the paraffin family and has excellent anti-detonation characteristics. Heptane, being a pure spirit, possesses poor anti-detonation properties. Therefore, iso-octane and heptane represent opposite ends of the octane scale, being equivalent to 100 and 0 octane respectively. The comparison test is carried out in a single-cylinder engine with a variable compression ratio, first developed by Harry Ricardo in 1912. (He also introduced the theory to differentiate between pre-ignition and detonation, which is still accepted by pilots today.) A fuel's octane rating number is obtained from the percentage of iso-octane present in the comparable iso-octane/heptane blend: since 100 octane is pure iso-octane, it follows that 87 octane fuel is equivalent to 87 per

The Piper PA-28 Cherokee line replaced the high-wing Tri-Pacer. Early 140 models used 87-octane fuel; the 160 model burned 100LL, while the later Cherokee Warrior required 100/130-octane fuel.

cent iso-octane, and so on. With the advent of fuels with better detonation characteristics than 100 per cent iso-octane, the octane rating numbers were no longer logical. This led to the introduction of the performance number system for classifying fuel.

As mentioned previously, a fuel's hydrocarbon composition determines its anti-detonation qualities, which can be increased by adding tetraethyl lead. The addition of TEL to fuel became necessary to prevent detonation in high-power engines, which require high-octane fuel, usually above 90 octane. The disadvantage of TEL is that it leaves lead deposits on the cylinder walls, and causes valves and valve seats to burn. This is where ethyl dibromide plays its part as a scavenging agent. It clears the cylinders of any unburnt lead and reduces the corrosive effects. The addition of lead to fuel is essential, but lead is bad for humans. Environmentalists around the world are pushing for lead to be removed from all fuels, hence the unleaded petrol used by modern motor vehicles. However, many of the world's light aircraft still need leaded fuel. In the 1970s, Shell introduced 100LL (low lead) fuel to partly alleviate this problem. At present, the highest octane rating achievable without lead is in the mid-90s.

The early types of low-power engine ran quite happily on low-octane fuel, having low compression ratios and low ignition temperature. During World

War 2, however, aircraft piston engines were developed to produce much more power, culminating in the post-war Wright Turbo Compound radial engine of 3,400bhp and other similar-sized engines. These high-power engines with their higher compression ratios, higher ignition temperatures and greater supercharger pressures were able to develop higher thermal efficiencies, resulting in greater power and relatively lower fuel consumption. For these engines, low-octane fuel was totally unsuitable, so higher-octane fuels were developed. These possessed greater anti-detonation properties. This required the octane rating scale to be extended beyond 100 and led to the double-figure performance number, 100/130 for example. The first and second numbers indicate the fuel's performance in lean and rich mixture settings respectively.

Each type of engine is designed to operate on fuel of a specific octane rating or performance number. If the octane rating is too low, the engine will suffer from overheating, burnt spark plugs, stuck valves, high oil consumption and, of course, a loss of power due to detonation. Conversely, using too high an octane rating can also cause damage to the cylinders along with other problems. Nevertheless, if the correct grade of fuel is not available, the rule is to use the next highest grade available as a temporary measure. However, with only 100 or 100LL and 100/130 being the most common Avgas on the market today, there is not much choice.

Octane rating should not be confused with specific gravity. While low-specific-gravity fuels have greater energy content, high-octane fuels produce greater horsepower for a given engine weight.

TYPES OF FUEL

All pilots should know the type of fuel used in the aircraft they fly and be familiar with their respective properties. The fuels and their properties are:

Avgas 100LL This is the most commonly used fuel in modern light aircraft engines. It is coloured blue and has a specific gravity of 0.72.
Avgas 100/130 Another common light aircraft fuel, 100/130 is coloured green and has a specific gravity of 0.714.
Mogas 91 (purple) or 96 (yellow) These fuels are only suitable for vintage, homebuilt and light sport aircraft. Use Mogas with caution and only when recommended.
Jet A-1 kerosene fuel Also known as Avtur or JP-1, this fuel may be clear or straw coloured and has a specific gravity of 0.80. It is only suitable for gas-turbine engines (turbo-prop, turbo-jet, turbo-fan, etc) and some of the aircraft diesel engines now appearing on the market. Never use Jet A-1 in a piston engine!

A Chronology of Fuel Development

Pre-1918   Fuel used before and during World War 1 was equivalent to only 50 octane (the octane scale had not been invented at that time). After the war, investigations were made into the effect of fuel quality on engine power in the USA and UK.

1919   Harry Ricardo of Cambridge University studied the knock resistance of various types of fuel. In the process, he discovered that the knock resistance of a fuel is proportional to its aromatic contents. The UK was the first country to establish knock-resistance standards for various fuels.

Thomas Midgeley, a Delco scientist in the USA, studied the problem of suppressing detonation by the use of aromatics, such as amines. In 1922, he also discovered the beneficial effects of adding tetraethyl lead and ethylene dibromide to fuel, which remains a common practice.

1924   The octane rating for fuel was increased to the equivalent of 73 octane.

1927   Graham Edgar, of the Ethyl Gasoline Company in the USA, established the octane rating system by blending iso-octane and heptane.

1928   Both the US Army and Navy started using the additive tetraethyl lead in their fuel. TEL allowed the octane rating to be increased up to 100 over the following few years.

1930   The US Army Air Corps and US Navy were the first to use 87-octane fuel, which they called 'fighting grade'.

1933   The airlines followed the trend set by the military in using 87-octane fuel.

1936   Fuel for US military aircraft was upgraded to 100 octane.

1937   The airlines stepped up to 90-octane fuel.

1939   100-octane fuel was specified for Bristol radial engines and other high-power British aero engines. Germany followed suit a year later.

1942   The Bristol engine manufacturer introduced double performance numbers: 100/130 for example. By adding 1.6 per cent of TEL and 2.5 per cent of methyl aniline to 100/130 fuel, the company created 100/150 fuel for such fighters as the North American Mustang.

1945   The airlines changed to 100-octane fuel (green). The US Air Force used 115/145 until the 1960s.

1970s   Shell Oil introduced 100LL (blue) Avgas in an attempt to reduce the amount of lead in aviation fuel, replacing 80/87 Avgas. Today, 100-octane or 100LL and 100/130 are the only major forms of fuel produced for piston-engine aircraft.

CHAPTER 2
AIRCRAFT FUEL
SYSTEMS

Aircraft fuel systems may be either of the simple gravity-feed type, as found on high-wing light aircraft, or of the pump-feed arrangement, as fitted to low-wing and more complex aircraft. The latter may have a multi-tank layout feeding two or more engines with a cross-feed system. Whatever the system installed in your aircraft, you should be totally familiar with its operation and peculiarities. Numerous accident investigations have proved that the pilots involved were not as familiar as they should have been with their aircraft fuel systems. A good working knowledge of the system in every type of aircraft you fly will ensure that you can handle the fuel in a correct and efficient manner to ensure a safe flight.

Depending on an aircraft's complexity, its fuel system may have some or all of the following: fuel tank, electric auxiliary pump, engine driven pump, tank vent and drain, quantity sensor, manual or electric primer, and carburettor or fuel control unit (FCU). More complex and multi-engine aircraft will have more than one of each item, and where there is more than one tank, there will be a tank selector and cross-feed (*see* Figures 2A and 2B). Also included are the instruments associated with fuel pressure, fuel quantity and fuel flow. Full details of an aircraft's fuel system can be found in the pilot's operating handbook (POH).

FUEL TANKS

Most light aircraft have one or two fuel tanks, but some types may have four. The third and fourth tanks may be outboard wing tanks, as found on the Piper PA 28/235 for example, or wing-tip tanks, as fitted to the Siai-Marchetti SF-260, and Cessna 310 and 402. Some POHs refer to these auxiliary tanks as reserve tanks, which, of course, hold an additional supply of fuel the main tanks. The wing-tip tanks on Cessna twins are canted upward. This, together with the wings' dihedral, places the tanks on a higher elevation than the engines. Presumably, gravity feed would keep the engines running in the unlikely event of a failure of both the engine driven and electric auxiliary fuel pumps. (No doubt, there is an aerodynamic advantage too, in the form of end plates that improve the wing's efficiency.)

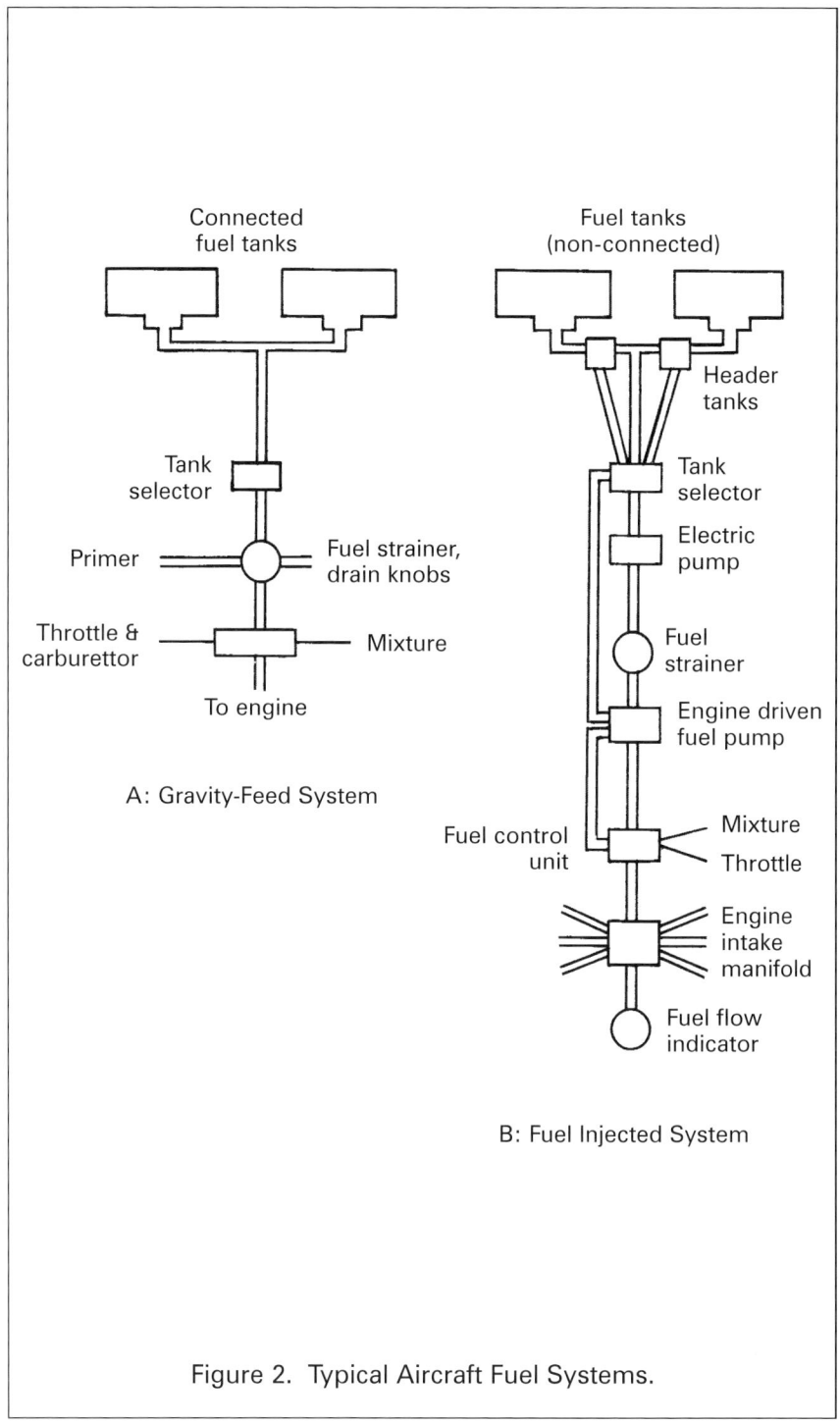

Figure 2. Typical Aircraft Fuel Systems.

Cessna twins are notable for their canted wing-tip fuel tanks. This example is the starboard tank of a Cessna 402.

Fuel tanks may be of the bag, rigid or integral type. The bag type, as found on the Victa Airtourer for example, is made of a flexible rubber material. The rigid tank is more common and is similar to a car fuel tank, being made as a separate unit and installed in the fuselage or the wing between pairs of wing ribs. The integral tank, which is normally found on large aircraft, is part of the wing's structure of ribs, spars and skins that has been sealed to make a fuel-tight compartment.

Figure 2A shows a simple gravity-feed fuel system, similar to that found in a typical high-wing aircraft. Fuel flows continuously due to gravity from both fuel tanks, which are permanently connected, via the 'on-off' tank selector, passing through the strainer to the carburettor. Fuel can be drained from the strainer or from the system drain plug.

Figure 2B shows a more complex system, of the type associated with a fuel injected engine. Fuel is contained in tanks that feed via header tanks to the tank selector. The electric auxiliary pump has a fuel bypass for when it is not running. The fuel continues through the strainer and engine driven pump to the fuel control unit and on to the intake manifold. The engine driven fuel pump provides a continuous flow under positive pressure. Vapour and excess fuel from the FCU and engine pump return via the tank selector to the reservoir tank of the selected main fuel tank.

It should be noted that these diagrams illustrate fuel systems in their basic forms for simplicity, and variations on these arrangements are possible.

The starboard wing-tip tank of a Siai Marchetti F260C, a four-seat, single-engine machine.

After examining the fuel vents during your pre-flight inspection, the next item to check is the quantity of fuel in the tanks. Make sure the fuel cocks are open before draining fuel for the fuel sample check. Otherwise, back pressure (lower air pressure in the tanks) can cause the fuel flowing from an open drain valve to stop. This could lead you to think that the valve is securely closed when, in fact, it is open. Later, the open valve would allow fuel to escape from the tank. Naturally, this would have a detrimental effect on your aircraft's range and endurance.

Be aware of the difference between usable, unusable and undrainable fuel. Any fuel below the fuel port inlet (to the engine) is considered to be unusable, and this is what is left in the tanks when they are run 'dry'. It should not be included when calculating usable fuel, the amount available for a flight. If you did include the unusable fuel, it could lead you to the mistaken belief that you had an extra fifteen minutes or so of flying time, with potentially disastrous results. A prolonged sideslip or any unbalanced flight attitude when the fuel quantity is low can cause the fuel to drain away from the inlet port, starving the engine of fuel. Some of the unusable fuel is undrainable fuel, which is the amount of fuel left in the tank's sump when it is emptied for maintenance.

Header tanks are small tanks located between the main tanks and the tank selector. Their purpose is to collect any excess fuel returned from the FCU or engine driven fuel pump.

FUEL TANK SELECTOR

The operation of a fuel selector can vary depending on the complexity of the fuel system installed in the aircraft. The more complex the system, the more options you have for setting the selector valve. This will have positions for turning off the flow of fuel, selecting individual fuel tanks or cross-feeding. A good knowledge of the tank selecting arrangement in your aircraft is essential for safe flying. In most light aircraft, the system will be quite simple and should present no problem in its operation, but this may not always be the case. Far too many pilots select tanks that are either empty or nearly empty, and quickly run out of fuel. Or they turn the selector to the 'off' position instead of selecting a tank with sufficient fuel for continued flight. Whenever you select a different tank, watch the fuel pressure gauge. A loss in pressure will soon become evident if the selector is not correctly positioned in the detent or if it is turned off. Make sure you have the correct end of the selector pointing at the chosen tank position. This may sound obvious, but some selectors point to the required tank with their short end, while others use the long end; it depends on the aircraft manufacturer's choice of style.

The most simple type of fuel system (gravity feed) usually has two interconnected tanks and a tank selector with only two positions: 'on' and 'off'. More common is the system with two individual tanks and a selector that gives the choice of 'off', 'both', 'left' or 'right'. With this arrangement, the pilot has the choice of running the system on both tanks simultaneously to simplify fuel management, or of selecting the left or right tanks individually to balance an uneven fuel load. A system with non-connected

The Cessna 414 was introduced in 1968 as a pressurized business and executive aircraft with canted tip tanks. Cruise speed is around 240kt (275mph) and range around 1,500n.miles (1,700st.miles). A later model, the Cessna 414 Chancellor, had a greater wingspan, but no tip tanks.

The Piper PA-24 Comanche was introduced in 1956 as a single-engine, four-seat aircraft. Various models were built, with engines from 180 to 400bhp, some with tip tanks (as here) and some without. Cruise speed and range varied with each model and engine. A twin-engine version was also built.

tanks offers the choice of 'off', 'left' or 'right'. An 'off' position is required in all systems to stop the fuel from flowing in the event of an engine fire. Multi-engine aircraft have a cross-feed facility as part of the tank selection arrangement. This is essential for transferring fuel to other tanks if one of the engines fails.

FUEL PUMPS AND PRIMERS

Most fuel systems require at least one engine driven fuel pump, which is mounted on the engine's accessory drive mechanism. An electrically driven centrifugal pump may also be part of the fuel system, particularly in low-wing aircraft and aircraft with fuel injected engines. The booster pump is provided to ensure that the fuel pressure supply to the engine remains above the working pressure.

In piston-engine aircraft, high temperature within the engine bay can cause vapour locks in the fuel lines and prevent fuel from flowing to the engine. Using the electric pump to purge the lines will stabilize the fuel pressure. Do not leave the pump turned on any longer than necessary, however, unless the POH dictates otherwise. The pump could overheat,

The Cessna 150/152 two-seat trainer has proved popular with flight training establishments worldwide. It has a range of over 350n.miles (400st.miles) with a cruise speed of 107kt (123mph) at 75 per cent brake horsepower. Endurance is up to 4hr 50min, depending on power settings. This is a 152 Aerobat.

adding to the high temperature within the engine bay. Opening the cowl flaps, increasing the mixture richness and increasing air speed (especially during a climb) can all help to cool things down under the cowl. Fluctuating fuel pressure accompanied by rough running is a sign of vapour in the fuel lines. In this situation, a precautionary landing may have to be considered.

The electric fuel pump should be used:

- To stabilize the fuel pressure (indicated by the fuel pressure gauge).
- To clear any vapour locks.
- For take-off and landing.
- During aerobatics or unusual attitudes.
- Whenever the engine driven pump is suspected of faulty operation.

In aircraft with fuel injected engines, electric auxiliary fuel pump switches may be of the split-rocker type, rather than the simple 'on-off' switches found with carburettor equipped engines. Make sure you know how to use the split-rocker type correctly; it can also be part of the priming system for engine starting. Misuse can cause the engine to flood, leading to a total engine stoppage or preventing the engine from starting. The right-hand side of the split-rocker switch provides 'off', 'low' and 'high' positions (the last two refer to fuel pressure). The 'low' setting is selected for normal engine starting and supplies fuel at low pressure to the FCU to prime the engine for starting. The 'high' position is used to purge the fuel lines of vapour during a 'hot' engine start. Engine flooding can occur if the switch is left in the 'high' position for too long. If this setting is selected during take-off, it can cause an over-rich mixture. This may keep the engine going until you retard the throttle to climb or cruise power, at which point the engine will stop due to the over-rich mixture. The left side of the rocker switch (marked 'maximum high') produces maximum fuel pressure and is only used for brief periods, such as when the engine driven fuel pump has failed or during the cruise phase of flight. Study the POH for the correct use of the auxiliary fuel pump switch in your aircraft.

In aircraft with carbureted engines, the fuel pressure should remain stable throughout all realms of flight. With a fuel injected engine, however, the fuel pressure is not only much higher, but also variable, depending on power setting and mixture/fuel flow chosen. Adjusting the mixture will affect the fuel pressure, as indicated by the fuel pressure gauge, which is calibrated to show fuel flow in gallons per hour and pressure in pounds per square inch. In either system, carburettor or fuel injection, a large drop in fuel pressure could indicate the failure of the engine driven fuel pump. This would be followed by engine failure due to fuel starvation while still running on a tank you believe has sufficient fuel. Check the fuel quantity gauges; you could be running a tank dry. A third possibility for a pressure drop, is a leak in the fuel lines. If you suspect this is the case, leave the throttle open and turn off the fuel with the idle cut-off mixture control. Closing the throttle can affect the airflow through the engine compartment (due to less prop wash), allowing the leaking fuel to come into contact with the hot exhaust system and ignite. Using the idle cut-off control will isolate the fuel from the engine compartment, after which you can turn off the fuel selector.

A fuel pressure that is higher than normal may be the result of back pressure caused by dirt in the fuel lines. The main problem here is the risk of the engine being flooded by excess fuel in the lines. This would be particularly dangerous if it occurred during take-off. Therefore, check the fuel pressure gauge for a normal reading, along with the other engine instruments, at the start of the take-off run. If the reading appears abnormal, abort the take-off immediately.

Priming an engine is a normal part of the start-up procedure, especially for a cold engine. If the engine has recently been in use, priming may not be necessary. Although the need for priming can vary from one aircraft to another, discretion is required. Use the primer only to assist starting. Primers on carburettor equipped light aircraft are usually of the manual plunger type, whereas fuel injected aircraft have an electrically operated device controlled by a rocker switch, as described previously.

Some aircraft engines do not have fuel primers at all. Priming is done by pumping the throttle.

FUEL DRAINS, STRAINERS AND VENTS

Aircraft fuel systems also include fuel drains, strainers and vents.

Fuel drains The fuel drains (also known as weather heads, drain points or drain cocks) are provided so that fuel samples can be drained from the system to check for water contamination. These are usually hand operated, spring loaded valves located in the bottom of each fuel tank sump.

Fuel strainers The fuel strainers are also known as fuel filters or gascolators. Their purpose is to filter out impurities in the fuel before it reaches the carburettor or fuel injection system and engine cylinders. They are placed in the fuel system's lowest points downstream of the tank outlets, fuel cocks and to the rear of the engine driven fuel pump.

Vents Each fuel tank is vented to atmosphere to allow air to enter the tank as fuel drawn from it and to provide positive air pressure above the fuel. This ensures a continuous flow of fuel to the engine. The vents also allow air and fumes to escape when the tanks are refilled by cross-feeding or when the fuel expands with rising temperature. It is important to check that the tank vents are clear during your pre-flight inspection, because a blocked vent reduces fuel flow to the engine, thus restricting range and endurance. A blocked fuel vent could also lead to a rigid type of tank collapsing due to the greater external air pressure. A collapsed tank could mislead you into thinking that you had refuelled the tank to its normal maximum capacity, when in fact it would only be partially filled due to its deformed condition. Obviously, carrying insufficient fuel for the flight will affect range and endurance. Another downside is the expensive repair bill!

CARBURETTOR AND FUEL CONTROL UNIT

The function of a carburettor is to mix fuel and air in the correct ratio for vaporization and burning in the engine's cylinders. The carburettor is calibrated for International Standard Atmosphere (ISA) conditions at sea level. When the aircraft climbs to altitude, due to reducing air temperature and pressure, the volume of ambient air drawn into the cylinders remains constant, but the mass (weight) reduces. To maintain the correct fuel/air ratio for all altitudes, the amount of fuel entering the carburettor must be reduced by means of the mixture control, preventing the mixture from becoming richer.

The manual mixture control is also used to stop the engine after flight by retarding it to the idle cut-off position. This action ensures that the cylinders are free of fuel, which serves two purposes. Firstly, with no fuel in the cylinders, the engine should not start inadvertently if someone leans on the propeller. Secondly, with no fuel present, there is less risk of corrosion forming in the cylinders. Fuel does remain in the carburettor's float chamber, however, ensuring an easy start-up for the next flight.

At high power settings above 75 per cent brake horsepower, the fuel

The simple fuel system of the DeHavilland DH-82 Tiger Moth consists of a single fuel tank located centrally between the two top wings. The cruise speed is a rather slow 78kt (90mph), giving it a range of 260n.miles (300st.miles). First flown in 1931, the Tiger Moth was operated by the RAF as a trainer aircraft. In later years, it saw service with aero clubs, top-dressing companies and private owners.

charge would cause unstable combustion, while at idle power, the inflow velocity would be too slow and the fuel charge would be retarded by friction in the inlet manifold. The auto-enrichment valve provides the richer mixture required at high and low power to alleviate these two problems. The carburettor also has an idling valve to ensure a continuous flow of fuel at idle power settings, when the suction through the venturi in the carburettor throat is reduced by the butterfly valve being almost closed. An accelerator pump operates as the throttle is opened fully, providing a small amount of extra fuel through the carburettor as the engine quickly accelerates to high power. Always open the throttle smoothly and steadily to avoid flooding and stalling the engine.

A fuel injected system has a fuel control unit in place of a carburettor. Its purpose is to meter the fuel supply to the engine in accordance with ambient conditions, limitations of the engine and, of course, pilot demand. The unit pumps a charge of fuel into the inlet manifold near the inlet valves, providing

The Champion 7EC Citabria has a simple fuel system. A transparent site gauge in each wing root indicates the fuel quantity. Citabrias flown by the author had no idle cut-off/mixture controls. Simultaneously turning off the magnetos and opening the throttle wide stopped the engine perfectly!

better fuel/air distribution to the engine for smoother running and quicker throttle response without flooding. The FCU is not affected by icing, although impact icing around the air intake could still be a problem. Cold engine starts are easier to achieve than with carburettor equipped engines. However, 'hot starts' can be harder to deal with, requiring a modified starting sequence. Vapour locks within the system are also possible, causing starting difficulties. In general, however, fuel injected engines are the better option of the two, providing smoother running and greater reliability.

FUEL QUANTITY SENSORS AND GAUGES

A fuel quantity sensor is located in each tank to transmit the fuel level in the tank to the fuel gauge in the cockpit. Two types of sensor are in common use: the capacitance type and the float type.

Capacitance fuel quantity sensors are usually found on jet transports, although a few piston-engine light aircraft have them as well. This type of sensor works on the principle of fluid (the fuel) changing the electrical characteristics of the sensor probes, being indicated as a quantity on the fuel gauge. The float type of fuel quantity sensor is more common to light aircraft. The movement of the float on the fuel's surface is transmitted via an electrical sensor to the fuel gauge. Although accurate, the float sensor is not as reliable as the capacitance type, due to the moving parts in the mechanism. Make sure that the master switch is on before checking electrically operated fuel gauges.

It is a common misconception among pilots that fuel gauges should be treated as unreliable instruments. However, it is imperative they are believed as much as any other instrument in the cockpit. They are more accurate than they are given credit for; if a gauge indicates a low fuel quantity, take that as being correct. Don't fly past an airport where fuel is available, thinking you have plenty of fuel on board when the gauges dictate otherwise. Remember that fuel gauges are inherently more stable in straight and level flight. Make a mental note of the gauge reading before refuelling, when refuelling is complete and after the flight. Do they indicate the amount of fuel that should be in the tanks? This will give you a good idea of their accuracy. Trust them; they could save you from a fuel mismanagement problem.

One last word on fuel gauges: be aware that most gauges, especially in American light aircraft, are graduated in US gallons, while fuel in other countries may be delivered in imperial gallons or litres. Take care not to confuse the different units when calculating fuel required and estimating fuel available. Remember that gauges show usable fuel. Most simply show fuel quantity as $1/4$, $1/2$, $3/4$ or full. A better system is the electronic type of read-out, which indicates numerically the actual amount fuel being used and the amount remaining.

Chapter 3
Fuel Management

In this chapter, we'll look into fuel management, covering refuelling the aircraft, checking quantities, in-flight fuel handling and finally the importance of engine oil. Having placed the required amount of fuel aboard the aircraft, it is a matter of using it wisely and efficiently.

REFUELLING

Airline pilots typically have their aircraft refuelled for them by the ground refuelling staff, although they are still responsible for the amount of fuel taken on board. The same applies for the pilots of light aircraft, although in some cases they may be required to perform the actual refuelling operation themselves, ensuring that the type of fuel required and quantity is correct. Refuelling is a simple enough operation, as long as a few common-sense procedures are followed to reduce the risk of fire.

- Before you start the refuelling process, check that the aircraft's brakes are on and that all switches and magnetos are off. Check that the fuel cocks are in their correct positions for refuelling. On some aircraft, fuel can flow between tanks during refuelling if the fuel cocks are set to 'both' or they are not turned off. After one tank has been filled, the fuel can drain from it into another tank while you fill the next tank, leaving the first tank with less fuel than you thought. This is why it is necessary to dip the tanks after refuelling. The problem can be avoided by turning the fuel selector to an individual tank. Some modern aircraft have single-point refuelling systems, where the fuel for all the tanks is added through one filler port. With such a system, allow time for the fuel to flow into the other tanks before you cease the refuelling operation.
- Make sure a fire extinguisher is readily to hand near the refuelling installation. Make sure you know where the extinguisher is located and how to operate it.
- Make sure your aircraft is a safe distance from buildings and other aircraft during the refuelling process. It should be at least 15m (50ft) from other aircraft or buildings. Make sure there is sufficient space to pull the aircraft clear if a fire breaks out.
- Passengers should not be on board the aircraft during the refuelling operation.

- Take note of the fuel gauge readings and compare them with the dipstick indication for each tank. Check the gauges again after refuelling as a cross-check on the amount of fuel aboard the aircraft. This will give a good indication of fuel gauge accuracy, or lack of it. Adding a given quantity of fuel, as read from the fuel pump installation, to what is believed to be in the tanks will help to determine the quantity on board, as will any fixed fuel-quantity marker within the tank itself.
- Make sure that the correct grade of fuel required by your aircraft will be delivered from the pumps. Do you require Avgas or Jet A-1?
- Do not smoke within 15m (50ft) of any aircraft being refuelled, and if a thunderstorm is in progress nearby, postpone refuelling until it has passed. The danger in the latter situation is the possibility, albeit slight, of lightning striking the refuelling installation or the aircraft. You should not be flying in the vicinity of a thunderstorm anyway, so there should be no hurry to refuel and get airborne.
- Cleanliness is important during all refuelling operations. Check that the fuel pump nozzle is clean; you don't want dirt dropping into your tanks. Refuelling from drums is not normally recommended, but sometimes this may be necessary, especially when operating from small airstrips. A clean chamois should be used to filter out any unwanted impurities that may have found their way into the fuel drums. A scrupulous check should always be made for water in the fuel after refuelling from drums;

A visit to the fuel pumps is a prerequisite of each flight.

condensation can quickly form in fuel drums that are left lying around in the open. This is less of a hazard when refuelling from an approved underground installation.

- Make sure that all fuel caps are securely replaced after refuelling. This may seem an obvious statement, but forgetting to refit filler caps can and does happen.
- Make sure you follow all company, aero club and civil aviation rules that relate to refuelling.

Dipping

After the aircraft has been refuelled, the tanks should be dipped as a final and accurate check on the quantity of fuel in the tanks. Dipping the tanks is not just a matter of poking the dipstick through the filler opening; a few precautions are in order:

- Do the readings on the dipstick indicate usable fuel? Make sure the markings on the dipstick are clear enough to read. If they are obscure, this could have a detrimental effect on determining the amount of fuel available for flight.
- The aircraft should be on level ground to ensure that the fuel tank is level when dipping, and the dipstick must be held vertically. If the ground is uneven, dip the tanks, noting the readings, then turn the aircraft around to face the other way. Dip the tanks again and take the average of the two readings. This will produce a more accurate reading than dipping the tanks only once.
- Dipsticks are specific to each aircraft and should not be used to dip the tanks of other aircraft, even if they are of the same type. Another aircraft of the same make and model may have different size fuel tanks installed. Therefore, the aircraft's registration should be printed on the fuel dipstick, and it should be used for that aircraft only.
- Compare the dipstick reading with the fuel gauges after dipping. This will give you an idea of the accuracy of the gauges.
- Due to a wing's dihedral, a wing mounted fuel tank will be on a slope, the amount depending on the aircraft type. High-wing types usually have less dihedral than low-wing aircraft, and wing thickness determines tank depth. The greater the dihedral and the thicker the wing, the easier it will be to judge the quantity of fuel in the tank.

Turbo-prop or Turbocharged?

As the pilot in command, it is your responsibility to ensure that refuellers place the correct quantity, type and grade of fuel aboard your aircraft. If the aircraft is turbocharged, this may be marked on the engine cowls. More than one refueller has confused the word 'turbocharged' with 'turbo-prop', however, and topped up the tanks of a piston-engine aircraft with Jet A-1 turbine fuel. Jet A-1 has a specific gravity of 0.80, which is heavier than Avgas

A Tomahawk's fuel quantity is measured by dipping the tanks.

at 0.72, so it will sink below any Avgas already in the tank, in much the same way as water settles to the bottom of the tank. Jet A-1 is a different type of fuel to Avgas and totally unsuitable for piston engines. Experience shows that it will run a piston engine for sufficient time to get airborne, at which point the engine will quit running. Range and endurance will then be measured in feet and minutes! Diesel engines, which can be run on Jet A-1, are now becoming available as retrofit options for Avgas drinking, piston-engine aircraft. Extra caution is required in such cases to ensure that the correct type of fuel is loaded aboard the aircraft to feed the diesel engine.

A method employed by some fuel suppliers to combat the risk of refuelling with the wrong type of fuel is to use different size fuel-pump nozzles for Avgas and Jet A-1. Avgas fuel-pump nozzles are between 40 and 49mm (1.57 and 1.93in) in diameter and fit easily into Avgas fuel-tank filler ports, which measure a maximum of 60mm (2.4in) in diameter. Jet A-1 fuel pump nozzles have a diameter greater than 60mm (2.4in) and some are squared off, not round, so they won't fit Avgas tanks. Caution is still required, however, as not all fuel suppliers use different sized fuel nozzles.

Fuel Tank Markings

As a further precaution, the American Petroleum Institute (API) introduced a system of colour coding decals on fuel pumps and aircraft fuel tanks. This

A Tomahawk is refuelled. Decals near the fuel filler indicate fuel type and grade, and tank capacity, removing the likelihood of confusion.

system should help alleviate any confusion over what type of fuel to load on board. The decals have the word 'Avgas' (and/or for example '100/130') in white letters on a red background, and 'Avtur' in white on a black background to indicate Jet A-1. Therefore, with colour coded decals in place and Jet A-1 fuel pump nozzles being too large for Avgas tanks, refuelling with the incorrect grade of fuel should never occur. Don't become complacent, however, check and double check.

Sensible Precautions

If the aircraft has auxiliary fuel tanks, these are normally refuelled first, unless the pilot's operating handbook (POH) dictates otherwise. Filling the auxiliary tanks first ensures that any impurities in the fuel supply end up in these tanks, not in the main tanks, which are normally used for take-off. Most light aircraft have their tanks located in the wings, with the filler holes and caps on the wing top surfaces, as opposed to transport-type aircraft, which are pressure filled from below the wings.

After refuelling, make sure that the fuel caps are replaced securely. A loose cap can allow rainwater to enter the fuel tanks and contaminate the fuel. Moreover, during flight, the reduced air pressure on top of the wing can suck fuel vapour from the tank.

A considerable amount of fuel can be lost in this way, as I discovered myself. A helpful gent offered to refuel my Citabria, but he failed to replace the fuel cap correctly. I should have checked that myself, but because he appeared to know what he was doing, I didn't bother. An hour into the flight, I noticed that the fuel gauge was reading low. I made a precautionary landing at the nearest airfield to check the fuel quantity, which was a lot lower than it should have been. I calculated that the fuel had been sucked out of the tank at the rate of 32ltr/hr (7imp.gal/hr or 8.5USgal/hr), which, combined with the fuel consumed by the engine, would have run the tanks dry before arrival at my destination, had I continued the flight.

Refuelling – Morning or Evening?

One important decision to be made is whether to refuel an aircraft at the end of the day's flying or before the first flight of the following day. There are advantages and disadvantages to both choices, so they must be considered with care.

Advantages of refuelling in the evening

- There will be less air space in the fuel tanks where condensation could form, or fumes collect that could be a fire hazard.
- It will remove the risk of the aircraft being flown on nearly empty tanks on the following day, and allow for an earlier departure.
- Any water or sediment in the newly added fuel will have time to settle in the tank drains overnight, ready to be discovered the following morning during the pre-flight inspection.

Disadvantages of refuelling in the evening

- The following day's payload may not be known. Too much fuel could be pumped into the tanks, requiring some to be drained off to maintain a safe, legal weight-and-balance situation.
- If the aircraft is not used the following day and is parked out on the ramp with rising daytime temperatures, the fuel could expand and overflow through the tank vents.
- The fuel could be stolen overnight.

Advantages of refuelling in the morning

- Cold fuel drawn from underground storage tanks will be denser than warm fuel, thereby producing greater power – and greater range and endurance. (Although this may not be much of a factor where light aircraft are concerned, it becomes more significant for large aircraft.)
- Knowing the payload, route and fuel requirement will allow the aircraft to be accurately refuelled with the necessary quantity of fuel.

Disadvantage of refuelling in the morning

- There is less time for any water or sediment to settle to the bottom of the tanks before carrying out the drain test.

In conclusion, it appears that morning refuelling is the better option. However, it is a matter of personal choice, and the decision should be taken after considering all the relevant factors.

Bonding

A discharge of static electricity during the refuelling process could cause a severe fire or even a fuel explosion. There are several causes of static electricity, such as air flowing over the aircraft in flight, dust blowing over the aircraft, fuel flowing through the refuelling hose (or chamois if refuelling from drums), and also nylon, Dacron or wool clothing.

Therefore, the aircraft must be grounded (or bonded, as it is called) to the fuel supply unit to dissipate any static electricity. This is done by attaching the grounding wire from the hose to the grounding clip on the aircraft, preferably before the fuel cap is removed. If there is no grounding clip on the aircraft, the grounding wire should be fixed to the neck of the refuelling port or some other clean, bare metal part of the aircraft, such as the exhaust pipe.

The bonding wire from the fuel-pump installation attached to the underwing ground clip.

Keeping the fuel nozzle in contact with the bare metal around the tank's filler port will equalize the electrical potential between aircraft and hose. When refuelling has been completed, if possible, the fuel cap should be replaced before disconnecting the grounding wire.

Static electricity

What we commonly refer to as static electricity is, in fact, electrical potential difference. Static electricity is the field of science concerning the imbalance of electrical charge voltage at rest, known as electrostatics.

Static electricity or, to be precise, potential difference is explained by the following. The molecules in the hydrocarbons of fuel are not normally very highly charged and are mixed together. As long as the positive and negative charged molecules are well mixed, there is no problem. When the fuel flows through the hose, however, the positive and negative molecules become separated. The former attach to the fuel and are carried along in the flow, leaving the negative molecules attached to the pipe. This causes a large potential difference – static electricity – with the ever present risk of a spark causing an explosion. This is where the grounding wire comes into play; it provides a path for the static electricity to make its way to earth, reducing the potential difference.

The risk of a spark from static electricity is always there to some degree, so always take the necessary precautions to prevent it. Use the grounding wire every time you refuel.

FUEL SAMPLING

After refuelling, the next step is to take a sample of fuel from each drain cock. Water and fuel won't mix together, and since water is denser than fuel, eventually it settles to the bottom of the tank. Draining a fuel sample allows you to ascertain if any water or contaminants are present in the fuel. Water can enter the tanks as condensation due to humidity, or as rainwater through leaking filler ports. Also, sediments can be present if the fuel is contaminated. Before sampling the fuel, give the wings a shake to free any trapped water droplets and allow them to sink to the fuel drains. A bladder tank can trap water in its low points or wrinkles at the bottom. If possible, after refuelling, wait a while to allow any sediments or water in the fuel to settle. If the aircraft has been parked outside in very cold temperatures, there is a possibility that any water present may have become frozen in the bottoms of the tanks or in the fuel drains, preventing the test from being completed until the drains have been cleared.

You should know the positions of all the fuel drains on your aircraft and the quantity of fuel that must be extracted to make a full check. Some fuel lines can be quite long and may require a considerable amount of draining before pure fuel, free of water and contaminants, flows from the drains. Examine each fuel sample for sediment, indicated by cloudiness, or globules of water. Fuel test papers and paste are also available for checking the presence of water.

Sediment could be present in the form of rust, sand or micro-organisms. The last will appear as a slimy brown substance, which can block fuel screens and filters. This is more common to turbine fuel than Avgas, and is more likely to form in conditions of high temperatures and humidity, such as in the tropics. If an excess of water has been drained out, you should discuss this problem with a ground engineer or chief pilot. Most sample cups are usually too small to accept an appropriately sized sample, so either take several samples using the clear plastic cup provided, or employ a larger container, such as a glass jar. Remember that all water and sediment must be removed before flight.

The colour of the fuel should also be checked to ensure that the correct grade is in the tanks. When checking the fuel, hold the sample cup against a background that contrasts with the fuel's colour. Checking 100LL (blue) against a blue sky will make any water present in the sample also appear blue. As a result, it could be mistaken for pure fuel. Instead, use the white of the fuselage as a background. Also, make sure you have sufficient light to inspect the sample properly. At night, use a white light source of sufficient strength for checking the sample. A final check is to take a quick sniff – does it smell like fuel or water? Don't overdo the smell test, however, since breathing in too many fumes can be a health hazard!

Some pilots claim that the fuel sample should not be returned to the tank. If the sample is found to be pure fuel, however, there is no reason not to return it to the tanks. Why waste it? Besides, throwing fuel on to the ground can soften asphalt, damage grass and be a potential fire hazard. Moreover, fuel spilt on to the aircraft's tires can cause deterioration of the rubber. If you do throw the fuel sample on to asphalt, watch what happens to it. If it evaporates, it is pure fuel; if it is water, it will form a small pool. Different fuels evaporate at different rates, which can vary with ambient temperature and humidity.

Throwing or spilling fuel on the ground can be hazardous to the environment. Some fuel will evaporate on the ground, while the rest will soak through to the soil below. Eventually, it will find its way into the drainage system, and possibly into drinking water supplies or agricultural irrigation systems – in short, a human health hazard.

Fuel sampling is an important part of the pre-flight inspection. It should be done with care and not be rushed. Make sure the drain valves are correctly closed to avoid any leakage. Any fuel not returned to the aircraft's fuel tanks should be disposed of in the correct manner.

PRIMING

It is normal practice to prime an engine before starting it, particularly for the first start of the day, when the engine will be cold and the fuel less volatile.

Taking a fuel sample to check for water contamination.

For the first start, three strokes of the manual primer are normally recommended; subsequently, two strokes should suffice. Priming delivers neat fuel into the induction manifold, carburettor or cylinder intake ports. Over-priming can deliver too much fuel into the cylinders and wash the lubricating oil from their walls, causing hard starting due to reduced cylinder compression. Remember that oil not only lubricates the moving parts, it also seals any gaps, preventing loss of compression. In addition, excess fuel dripping back into the carburettor could be ignited by a backfire, resulting in an induction fire. Priming is best done just prior to operating the starter; if it is left too long, the vaporized fuel will become liquid fuel again.

Unless otherwise specified in the POH, do not prime the engine with the throttle – this is bad airmanship. It could start an induction fire more readily than over-priming with the primer control. With some types of carburettor, excess air can be forced into the cylinders when pumping the throttle to prime the engine. This could result in hard starting due to the mixture being too lean. In carburettors with updraught or side-draught induction, the fuel flows upward or sideways. Pumping the throttle provides a coarse mist of fuel that will not vaporize correctly and may not continue flowing to the engine.

It could then drip back down into the induction system, forming a pool of liquid fuel that would be a fire hazard. The correct use of the fuel primer safely provides the fine atomized mist essential for easy starting.

Despite the foregoing, and as strange as it may sound, some aircraft engines do not have fuel primers. Pumping the throttle does the priming. Check in the POH.

After priming the engine, make sure that the primer control is securely locked in the closed position. If not, it could creep open in flight, allowing excess fuel to enter the cylinders, which would increase the richness of the mixture and possibly cause an engine failure. Remember, if the fuel/air ratio is too rich, it won't burn efficiently enough to generate power.

FUEL FLOW CHECK

One of the pre-flight checks is to ascertain that fuel is flowing freely from all of the tanks. Before take-off, the engine should be run for at least one minute from each tank in turn. This will verify that the tank, and its fuel lines and pumps are all feeding freely. If a cross-feed system is installed, this too should be checked prior to take-off.

If the aircraft has two fuel tanks, taxi to the holding area on one tank (use the tank with the lowest amount of fuel if they contain different quantities), and switch over to the other tank for the engine run-up and take-off. It is important that the take-off is always made using the same tank as that selected for the engine run-up, and with the greatest amount of fuel. You will then know for certain that the tank will deliver sufficient clean, uncontaminated fuel for the high-power required for take-off. After lining up on the runway, apply full power and check the engine rpm, manifold pressure, fuel flow (or fuel pressure), engine temperatures and pressures to assure yourself that everything is in order. An engine failure on take-off due to fuel starvation will quickly terminate your flight, having an adverse affect on range and endurance.

If the cross-feed system has been selected to balance the tanks, monitor it constantly. Many a pilot has been distracted with other cockpit duties while all the fuel in one tank is transferred to another.

IN-FLIGHT FUEL HANDLING

In most aircraft, the fuel tanks are located in each main wing, so the fuel must be drawn evenly from each tank in turn to maintain lateral trim. Some high-wing aircraft have a gravity feed from both tanks at once, simplifying fuel handling in flight. The majority of low-wing aircraft, however, require one tank to be used at a time. This leads to frequent tank changing to prevent uneven weight distribution across the wingspan. A good time to make the first tank change is at the top of the climb as you enter the cruise. Then switch tanks every twenty or thirty minutes. When auxiliary fuel tanks are fitted, the normal practice is to use these tanks first during cruise flight, followed by the main tanks. In transport aircraft, however, especially those with sweptback wings, this may not be possible. Depending on the aircraft's design, it may be necessary to use certain inboard or outboard tanks first to keep the centre of gravity within limits. It all boils down to knowing your aircraft's fuel system.

The quantity of fuel carried in light aircraft is relatively small, but the fuel's weight becomes more significant in larger aircraft where the cabin load is restricted to a given weight. This is known as the zero fuel weight (ZFW). Any additional weight added to the aircraft must go into the fuel tanks. The reason for this is that the wings can only carry a certain amount of weight in the fuselage without placing too much stress on the wing roots. Imagine two men standing on the middle of a plank of wood that is supported at each end – the plank will bend downward in the middle. An aircraft with a heavy cabin load and light wings would experience the same effect. All of the weight would be in the middle of the wingspan, placing great stress on the wing attachment points. Wings that are heavy with full fuel tanks are less prone to bending due to cabin load, the total weight being distributed across the wingspan. A secondary advantage is that less flexible wings guarantee a smoother ride in turbulence. Consequently, using the inboard tanks before the outboard tanks will help to alleviate wing bending stress. That said, a sufficient quantity of fuel must remain in the main tanks for landing, or a go-around or diversion.

Running the Tanks Dry

When the tanks are low on fuel, avoid unbalanced flight, such as sideslipping; this could uncover the fuel tank outlet and starve the engine of fuel. Some aircraft have a time limit for carrying out such manoeuvres as sideslips. Again, this will be in the POH.

If, toward the end of a flight, one tank has only a quarter of its fuel remaining, run the other tank to nearly empty before changing back to the quarter-full one for the remainder of the flight and the landing. Whenever you change fuel tanks in flight, make sure you turn the selection lever to the correct position by actually looking at it. Monitor the fuel pressure gauge for any drop in pressure, and turn on the fuel pump if required. This will verify that fuel is being delivered from the newly selected tank and that there is no blockage. A fuel pressure drop followed by the engine dying will indicate that you have run a tank dry. The propeller will continue to windmill for some time after the loss of power, whereas a mechanical failure would cause the engine to stop suddenly. Change tanks immediately and use the boost pump as recommended in the POH.

The American FAA (Federal Aviation Adminstration) regulations for aircraft certification require that when a tank is run dry, power should be regained within ten seconds for a single-engine aircraft, and twenty seconds for a multi. In most cases, however, a carburettor equipped engine will restart

The Miles Messenger M-38 was developed in 1942 for the Royal Air Force as a liaison aircraft. Ex-military types, such as this, have become popular in private ownership. The Messenger has a relatively short range of 400n.miles (460st.miles) with a cruise speed of around 110kt (126mph).

within one or two seconds, while a fuel injected unit will take six to eight seconds. That said, an engine could be difficult to start if air has entered the fuel lines – and very difficult to start if there is no fuel in the tanks!

Running a tank dry in flight will be a memorable experience, a practice you won't want to repeat too often. Besides, if you have got to the point in flight where you are running tanks dry to make your destination airport, then your pre-flight planning and in-flight fuel handling need positive attention. This is pushing your range and endurance to the limit, and is definitely not good airmanship. It has been known for pilots to run a tank completely dry and suffer an engine failure when the other tank was full of fuel. In this situation – one tank empty and one tank full – the aircraft would be unbalanced laterally, and it is difficult to imagine how this could go unnoticed by the pilot, since the heavy wing would want to drop all the time instead of remaining level. Using the fuel logically from each tank in turn maintains lateral balance and assures continued flight. Keeping a written fuel log helps maintain track of the fuel situation. It's basic airmanship.

STARVATION AND EXHAUSTION

No, I am not talking about an underfed and overworked pilot! I'm referring to the aircraft's fuel status. Fuel starvation and exhaustion are frequently mentioned in aircraft accident reports. In one year, the American National Transportation Safety Board (NTSB) recorded 2.7 per cent of accidents being attributed to fuel starvation and 6.4 per cent to fuel exhaustion. Both problems are due to poor airmanship or flight planning, and neither should ever occur. This is one cause of accidents that could be completely removed, if pilots were more vigilant in their piloting techniques.

You may be wondering how fuel starvation differs from fuel exhaustion. I'll explain.

Fuel starvation occurs when:
- The fuel tank selector is turned to the 'off' position or to an empty tank.
- A blockage or water is present in the fuel lines or fuel strainers.
- The tank vent is blocked, restricting fuel flow.
- The mixture control is moved to the 'idle cut-off' position when the carburettor heat should have been applied.
- Carburettor icing forms.
- The engine fuel pump fails.
- The primer is not locked in the closed position after priming the engine before flight. (This will enrich the fuel/air mixture and flood the engine, causing rough running and a loss of power.)

Fuel exhaustion occurs when:
- No usable fuel is left in the tanks. This is due to poor fuel handling or flight planning
- Delays or diversions due to weather prolong the flight.
- Errors are made in converting fuel amounts from one unit to another.
- Fuel gauges give incorrect readings.

It's as simple as that, and neither should ever happen. Correct fuel handling on the ground and in the air is essential to ensure fuel-efficient flight; it is a very important part of aircraft handling and airmanship.

ESSENTIAL OIL

Just as an engine requires a constant flow of fuel to keep it running, it also needs a constant flow of lubricating oil at sufficient pressure to maintain its health. Without oil circulating through its vital parts, an engine would overheat and very quickly seize up, terminating a flight well short of its true range and endurance. Oil is essential for engine cooling, cleaning and lubrication. Not only does it help carry away engine heat, but it also deposits a film of oil on the cylinder walls. This helps the compression rings to seal the gaps between the pistons and walls, preventing blow by of the compressed gases in the combustion chambers. Oil reduces power loss due to friction, and general wear and tear throughout an engine. Condensation can form inside an engine during the day as it cools between flights, allowing water to settle and form rust, which in turn can reduce engine life. As the oil circulates through an engine, it removes any rust that may have formed. Therefore, using oil with a good rust inhibitor is vital.

Most modern light-aircraft engines utilize a wet-sump lubrication system, the oil supply being contained within the engine's sump, from where it is circulated around the engine; a dry-sump system has a separate reservoir for the oil. The oil is transferred from the sump by means of a pump, correct pressure being maintained by a pressure regulator. On its journey around the engine, the oil passes through a filter to extract any solid particles it may have picked up, and through an oil cooler, normally cooled by the airflow, before it returns to the sump. Oil temperature and pressure gauges complete the lubrication system, informing the pilot of its health, so keep an eye on these gauges during flight.

The correct grade and type of oil should be selected, following the engine manufacturer's recommendations. This could be a single grade of oil of around SAE 50 for ambient temperatures of 5°C (41°F) and higher, but for colder temperatures, lower-viscosity oil will be required. The SAE rating is based on the Saybolt viscosity test used by the oil manufacturer. You may also come across oil with a higher rating number, such as 100 grade. This is a commercial aviation number, double that of its equivalent SAE rating. In other words, 100 grade is the same as SAE 50. An alternative choice is oil with a multi-viscosity rating, commonly known as multi-grade oil, for example, 10W30. This type of oil remains thin enough for quick and easy engine starting, but becomes thicker and won't break down at high engine temperatures. Due to its higher rate of flow, multi-grade oil will run cooler in the engine. It also helps reduce oil and fuel consumption, and lasts well between oil changes. Using oil of a lower grade (lower viscosity) than recommended may not provide the required lubrication. Similarly, if the oil grade is higher than specified, it will be too thick to circulate freely around the engine.

Aero engine oil can be divided into two basic types: non-detergent mineral oil and ashless dispersant oil. The former is made from a kerosene base, while the latter is produced from synthetic oil refined from crude oil. Both types are commonly used in aircraft. Prior to 1958, the only type of oil available was mineral oil. Since then, however, the oil companies have made great advances in lubricating oil technology, and now a variety of different types are available. Today's mineral oil is used mainly for breaking in new engines or engines that have been overhauled, where minute particles of dirt or metal have been left behind in the engine and assist in honing the cylinders. After the engine has been run for 25–50 hours, the oil is changed for an ashless dispersant (detergent) type for general daily use. Its dispersant characteristics

The P-3C Orion was developed from the 1959 civilian Lockheed Electra four-engine turbo-prop airliner as a long-range, maritime patrol aircraft. It has a basic endurance of twelve hours, which can be extended to seventeen hours with two engines shut down.

flush out the dirt and metal particles to help keep the engine oil clean. This oil also has better thermal stability and enhanced oxidation properties.

Always make sure that the correct grade of oil is used when topping up your aircraft's engine prior to flight, otherwise serious engine damage could result. Never mix mineral oil with ashless dispersant oil; each type of oil is used for a specific purpose.

A healthy aero engine will use relatively little oil. For example, a 150hp Lycoming engine, as found in a Cherokee 140, consumes as little as 0.09ltr (0.16pt) of oil per flying hour. It is imperative to check the oil quantity with the dipstick prior to each flight to ensure that there is sufficient in the engine. A minimum quantity must be in the engine's sump to provide the necessary oil pressure for lubrication and engine cooling, and allow for oil consumption during the flight. When the engine is running, insufficient oil can be indicated by low or fluctuating oil pressure, followed by the engine overheating and eventually total failure. Overfilling the sump, can result in excess oil being blown out through the breather pipe and being wasted, not to mention making a mess.

Check the oil pressure as soon as the engine starts, confirming that it rises to the normal operating pressure within thirty seconds. If the pressure does not rise, shut down the engine immediately to prevent damage. It is also good practice to check the oil pressure gauge along with the other engine instruments at the start of the take-off run, and at frequent intervals throughout the flight. In fact, whenever you make a power change is a good time to check all the engine instruments.

Oil temperature and pressure must remain within limits at all times. If the temperature is too low, any water from condensation inside the crankcase will not vaporize during flight. Even if the oil temperature gauge is reading 'in the green', this may not be a high enough temperature; a minimum of 82–85°C (180–185°F) is required. A normal temperature combined with a drop in pressure indicates a faulty oil pressure gauge or relief valve. In this case, a landing should be made as soon as possible at the nearest airport to have it checked. The worst situation is a total loss of oil pressure with an associated rise in oil temperature. This is a sign that the engine is about to quit due to a lack of oil. Throttle back to idle and carry out a forced landing immediately, using engine power only if absolutely necessary to ensure a safe landing. If you are flying a multi-engine aircraft, you have the option of shutting down the engine completely while you head for the nearest suitable airport. Without oil in the engine, your aircraft's range and endurance will be quickly and dramatically cut short. Oil in the engine is just as essential as fuel in the tanks.

If you ensure that the correct type and quantity of engine oil is used, and apply common sense airmanship in handling the engine, you should alleviate any engine problems that could compromise range and endurance.

Chapter 4
Leaning
Techniques

For fuel to be burned in an engine's cylinders, it must be combined with air. Air is not a gas in its own right; it consists of a combination of several different gases. The two main gases are oxygen and nitrogen. Oxygen from the ambient air is mixed with the hydrocarbons in the fuel as they pass through the carburettor (or fuel control unit of a fuel injected engine) to produce a combustible fuel/air mixture for delivery to the engine's cylinders. The engine manufacturer will calibrate the carburettor to run rich at sea level, at a temperature of 15°C (59°F). However, because aircraft operate at various altitudes, where the air is thinner, leaning the fuel/air mixture becomes a very important part of fuel handling and engine operation. The correct richness of the mixture is essential to prevent pre-ignition and detonation (*see* Chapter 1).

The Advantages of Leaning

Maintaining a constant fuel/air ratio has several advantages, particularly from an aircraft engineer's point of view, notably:

- Cooler cylinder head temperatures.
- Cleaner combustion chambers (due to fewer hydrocarbons).
- Cleaner oil.
- Lower fuel consumption.

However, engine manufacturers may recommend not running at lean of peak cylinder head temperatures, because excessive leaning can cause:

- Chemical changes in the form of lead oxybromide deposits, resulting in pre-ignition.
- Possible damage to connecting rods.
- Damage to main bearings.
- Burned valves.

Therefore, running an engine rich of peak temperature is the best option. Although fuel flow increases by 3–4 per cent rich of peak, this is cheaper than the cost of an engine repair or a forced landing. This point becomes even more relevant with engines of high horsepower. The pilot's operating handbook (POH) for the Cessna 207's 300bhp Continental fuel injected engine, for example, does not authorize operating the engine at any exhaust gas temperature within 18°C (25°F) or lean of peak temperature at any time. In other words, the engine must always be operated on the rich side of peak temperature. However, leaning the mixture to some degree is essential for increasing an aircraft's range and endurance.

FUEL/AIR RATIO CHARTS

The fuel/air ratio charts in Figures 3 and 4 illustrate several important facts in respect of leaning the mixture. On the right of Figure 3, above a fuel/air ratio of 0.08, the mixture is too rich to burn efficiently. When the mixture is leaned, we move across the charts from right to left, passing the best power setting at rich of peak (RoP) – the maximum temperature – to the best economy setting at a point lean of peak (LoP). This diagram shows the change in cylinder head temperature (CHT) and exhaust gas temperature (EGT) as the mixture is leaned from a full rich setting to best power, or by further leaning to best economy. The fuel/air ratio of 0.08 means 0.08lb of fuel for each pound of air.

Notice on the left side of the chart that the CHT is marked in degrees Centigrade, while the EGT is given in degrees Fahrenheit.

RICH MIXTURE

As already mentioned, a rich mixture is required to prevent pre-ignition and detonation. At the correct fuel/air ratio, the carbon monoxide within the fuel combines with oxygen to produce carbon dioxide and releases sufficient heat to produce power. When the mixture is too rich (greater than a fuel/air ratio of 0.074), there is insufficient oxygen to combine with the excess fuel to form carbon dioxide and produce power. Some unconsumed matter is discharged through the exhaust and is evident as black smoke. A quantity of the excess fuel helps to cool the cylinders, but if the mixture is too rich, fuel is wasted, cutting range and endurance. Consequently, the mixture must be maintained within certain limits to function correctly, specifically a fuel/air ratio of 0.06–0.08.

The degree of richness depends on the power setting; it must be richer at full throttle to prevent pre-ignition, detonation and overheating of the cylinders, and to aid engine cooling during the initial climb to altitude. The excess fuel in a rich mixture helps cylinder cooling by absorbing latent heat through vaporization. Throttling back an engine during the climb does not help it run cooler, because the cylinders are deprived of the extra fuel used for cooling. Better engine health is achieved at full throttle with a fixed-pitch propeller. Note that a 300bhp engine uses fuel at the rate of 9ltr/hr

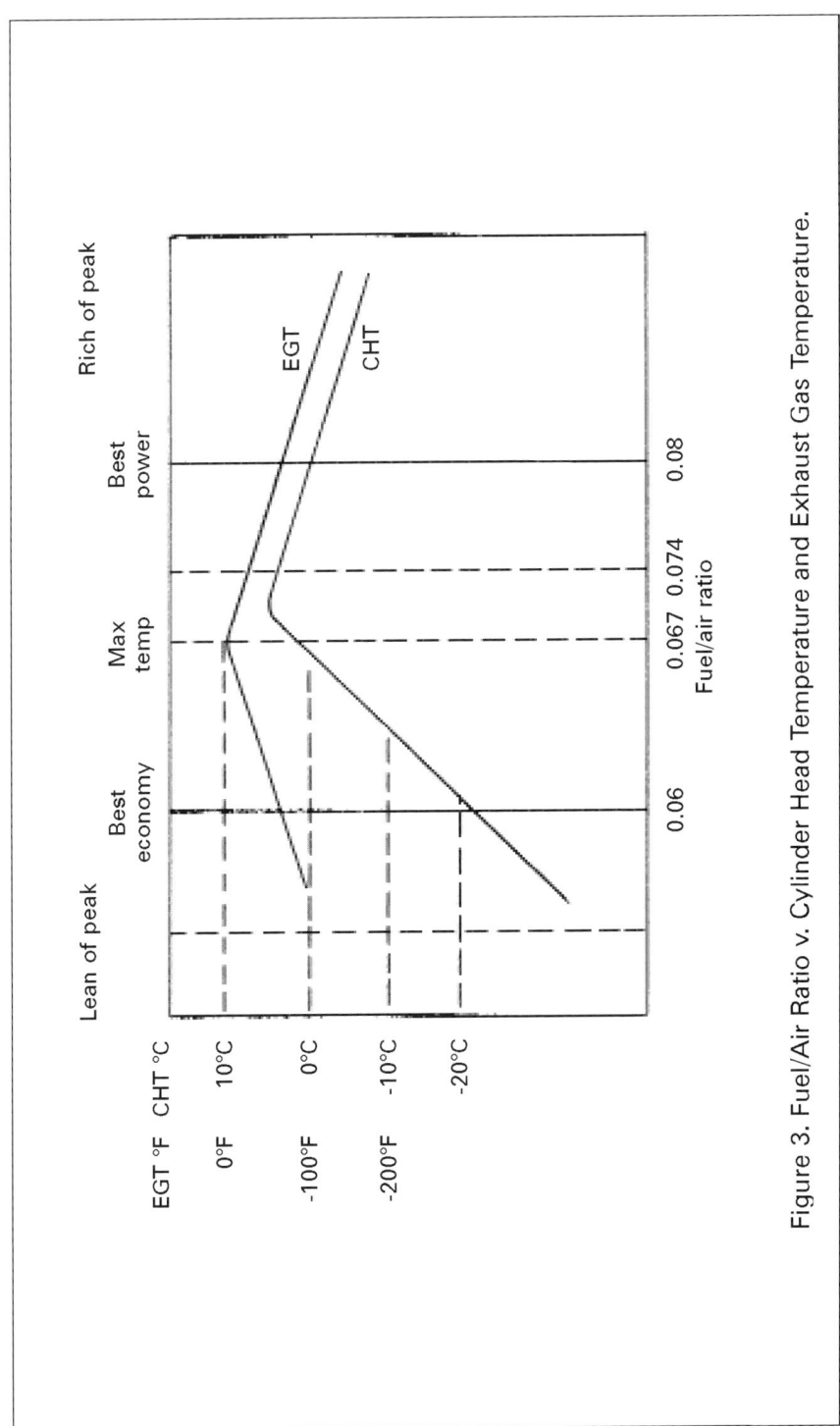

Figure 3. Fuel/Air Ratio v. Cylinder Head Temperature and Exhaust Gas Temperature.

(2imp.gal/hr or 2.4USgal/hr) for cooling purposes during the climb. At low power settings, the engine quickly cools, robbing the fuel of the heat required for vaporization. This leaves some heavier fuel elements still in a liquid state and with insufficient fuel vapour for complete combustion. The reduced air flow velocity through the carburettor could be insufficient to produce a uniform mixture distribution to each cylinder, resulting in a fuel/air ratio that is either too lean or too rich. In this situation, a rapid application of throttle could easily stall the engine, which is the last problem you want during take-off, or when executing a missed approach or overshoot. For these reasons, the carburettor is set to run richer at high and low power settings, and leaner during the cruise to save fuel (*see* Figure 4).

BEST POWER

Figure 3 indicates that a fuel/air ratio between 0.074 and 0.08 covers the best power range. A ratio of 0.08 rich best power is required for 100 per cent maximum except take-off (METO) engine power, and leaning to 0.074 lean best power produces maximum power for a particular engine speed (rpm). Further leaning below 0.067 will produce less power, as indicated by Figure 4. Some large engines can produce greater power for a limited time during

A Douglas DC-3 freighter is refuelled from a tanker while being prepared for its next flight.

An Embraer Bandeirante is refuelled from underground tanks with the help of a mobile pump cart. This aircraft has a maximum range of 1,100n.miles (1,250st.miles), cruising at 10,000ft with a thirty-minute reserve of fuel.

take-off and will require a greater fuel/air ratio of 0.08 to suppress detonation. At a ratio of 0.08 best power, a fixed-pitch propeller will attain its maximum rpm. If an EGT gauge is mounted on the instrument panel, it should indicate 32–65°C (90–150°F) on the rich side of peak temperature, but more about this later.

The combination of reduced power and increased air speed tends to cool an engine quite quickly, so closing the cowl flaps just prior to levelling off from the climb will help maintain a stable engine temperature. Waiting a couple of minutes will allow the CHT and EGT to stabilize before they are used for reference purposes when leaning the mixture. During the descent, the mixture should be leaned close to the best power setting to help keep the cylinders warm. Keep the lean setting for as long as possible during the descent down to circuit height, but be prepared to enrich the mixture if the engine begins to run rough and before increasing engine power. Remember that it is necessary to readjust the mixture whenever a power or altitude change is made. You need to use discretion in this respect. Always select a fully rich mixture for take-off, unless the engine manufacturer recommends leaning at hot and high-altitude airports to avoid rough running and a loss of power.

MAXIMUM TEMPERATURES

The fuel/air ratio range of 0.067–0.070 is known as the ideal mixture, being chemically correct because no fuel or oxygen remains after combustion in the cylinders. To be precise, the ratio of 0.067 is known as the stoichiometric mixture (from Greek, meaning in proportional amounts). The cylinder head and exhaust gas temperatures will reach their peak values at the ideal mixture setting, when there is an attendant reduction in fuel flow and a decrease in true airspeed of 2–3kt (2.3–3.5mph), from best rich power. The benefit is a saving in specific fuel consumption (SFC) as indicated in Figure 4.

Figures 3 and 4 illustrate the changes in temperature, fuel flow and specific fuel consumption. From the best power setting, the cylinder head temperature is zero degree referenced, and the temperature increases slightly when leaned to peak CHT at the fuel/air ratio of 0.067. With further leaning to best economy, the temperature decreases to approximately 15°C (59°F) below the initial zero degree reference at 0.06 ratio.

The chart shows a similar trend for the EGT, starting in this example at 24–38°C (75–100°F) rich of peak at the best power setting, and with the temperature increasing to its maximum value (zero degree reference) at a fuel/air ratio of 0.067 at peak EGT. Further leaning lowers the temperature to around 10–24°C (50–75°F) at best economy.

Figure 4 shows the variation in brake horsepower and SFC with a change in mixture setting. Again, with the mixture being leaned from full rich, the power, speed and fuel flow all decrease. With a best power setting at a fuel/air ratio of 0.074 and full rich mixture, maximum power is produced with an SFC at its upper limit. Leaned to peak temperature, the power falls to around 97–98 per cent, but with the advantage of the SFC reducing considerably to 90 per cent of the best power figure. Further leaning to best economy shows a decrease in power to around 88 per cent of best power, with SFC decreasing to around 88 per cent of the best power level.

LEANING IN THE CLIMB

When the aircraft climbs to altitude, the fuel/air ratio by volume remains constant. However, the fuel/air ratio by weight decreases with increasing altitude. Weight is the important factor in this situation, the weight of fuel required remaining constant with constant fuel flow. Because air density decreases with altitude (at 18,000ft, it is approximately 500hPa or mb, half the sea level value), the weight of air required also decreases. Eventually, this causes the fuel/air ratio to change, the mixture becoming richer as the aircraft climbs. This produces a reduction in power and a drop in engine speed. The engine of an aircraft with a fixed-pitch propeller will begin to run rough, while there will be a loss in manifold pressure if the aircraft is equipped with a constant-speed propeller. For this reason, the mixture must be leaned during the climb.

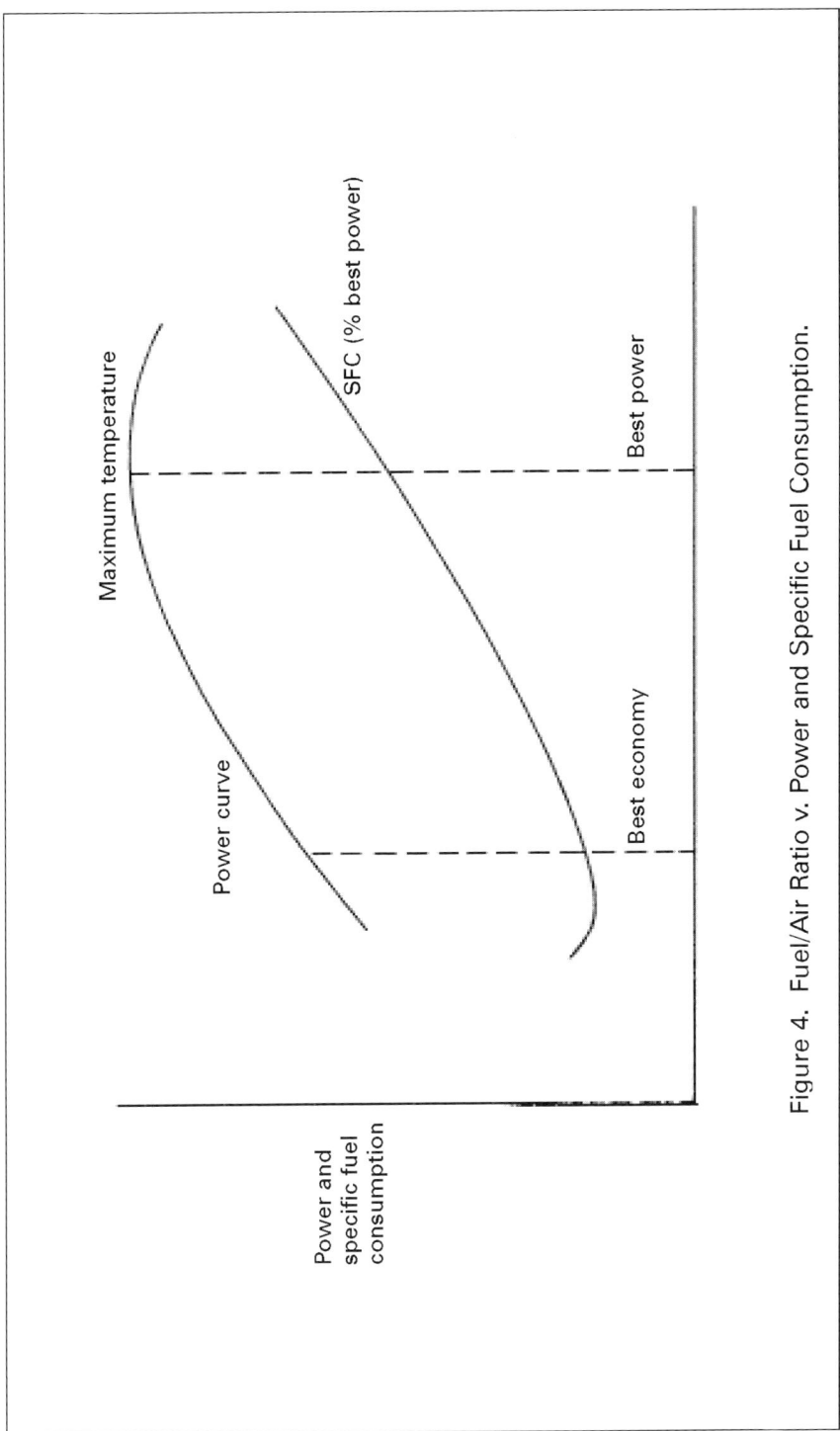

Figure 4. Fuel/Air Ratio v. Power and Specific Fuel Consumption.

BEST ECONOMY

For the engine to operate efficiently and economically, it is imperative that the fuel/air ratio is set to the best economy value of 0.06. This gives a drop in fuel consumption, hence the name of the setting. This should be selected for cruise flight to extend range and endurance if permitted by the POH, otherwise use peak CHT or EGT.

It is essential to choose the correct mixture setting for the stage of flight: rich for take-off and climb, lean for cruise and descent. Whether or not the mixture should be leaned during the climb depends on the aircraft type and pilot experience. For low-time pilots flying light aircraft with fixed-pitch propellers on short cross-country flights, the POH may recommend fully rich for climbing and cruise flight below 5,000ft density altitude. This is an old rule of thumb that dates back to the time of the early piston-engine airliners. With the advent of larger, more powerful engines mounted on aircraft flying international routes (DC-7s, Constellations, etc), leaning techniques became more refined to help stretch their range. This was essential, for example, on westbound transatlantic flights against strong headwinds. Nevertheless, leaning is related mainly to an engine's power output and not necessarily to its altitude. This means that an engine can be leaned at any altitude from sea level, provided the power output is below 75 per cent brake horsepower. Moving up to high-performance singles and light, twin-engine aircraft operating on long flights at higher altitudes, using the correct leaning procedure for the aircraft type becomes very important. Up to 14 per cent of fuel can be wasted if an engine is run at full rich and not leaned correctly, resulting in a reduction of an aircraft's true range and endurance, which in turn increases the cost of operating the aircraft.

I have made several references to percentage power, for example, 75 per cent brake horsepower. This is an arbitrary reference, because it can refer to 75 per cent of maximum take-off power (say 300bhp) or it can refer to 75 per cent of maximum cruise power (say 285bhp). The aircraft's POH will give a choice of power settings, fuel flows and airspeeds at various percentages of power. To the pilot, it does not really matter if it refers to maximum take-off power or cruise power; the important point is to adjust the power settings of rpm and manifold pressure as required, in accordance with the POH or flight manual.

TOO LEAN

In Figure 3, it can be seen that when the mixture is too lean (below 0.06), it will not produce power. This is due to the fact that a lean mixture burns too slowly. As a result, combustion is not complete until after the piston has passed top dead centre, which gives insufficient time for the manifold pressure to rise to its maximum level and produce its full power potential. When all the fuel is burned, some oxygen remains. This causes overheating

A De Havilland DHC-2 Beaver is refuelled with Avgas from a small tanker trailer at a rural airstrip.

of the cylinders and exhaust valves because the gas is still burning when the exhaust valves open. The results are:

- Rough engine running.
- Detonation and/or pre-ignition.
- A general loss of power.
- Possible engine damage.

LEANING METHODS

Basically, five different references can be used when adjusting the mixture, depending on the instrumentation installed on the aircraft's panel. These are:

- The manual method.
- The fuel flow gauge.
- The cylinder head temperature gauge.
- The exhaust gas temperature gauge.
- The exhaust gas analyser.

It must be remembered that maximum range, as quoted in the aircraft's flight manual, will be based on the mixture being leaned for 75 per cent brake horsepower or less.

The Manual Leaning Method

The manual method of leaning the mixture is suitable for any light aircraft with a carburetor equipped engine driving a fixed-pitch propeller. While flying at a constant speed, note the engine rpm and lean the mixture until the rpm reading increases to its peak value. This will occur at the correct fuel/air ratio for best power, which will produce the maximum true airspeed at that power setting. Further leaning beyond peak rpm to the onset of engine roughness, or the point when the engine speed starts to drop, will give the best economy mixture setting. This should be used for the cruise and descent. At the onset of rough running, the mixture should be enriched by pushing in the mixture control by about 5mm (0.25in). This will protect any cylinder that may already be running too lean due to uneven fuel distribution from the inlet manifold and poor flame propagation in the combustion chambers.

There are arguments for and against leaning to the onset of roughness. If the engine starts to run rough during the descent (or even in the cruise for that matter), enrich the mixture sufficiently to clear the roughness, going to full rich in the circuit or when level at a lower altitude. The argument against

A BAe Jetstream 41, the stretched-fuselage version of the Jetstream 31, takes on another load of Jet-A fuel.

Jet-A fuel is transferred from a tanker to a Jetstream 31.

leaning to the onset of roughness takes account of the uneven mixture distribution between the cylinders. If one of the cylinders is already running too lean, reducing the richness of the mixture further could lead to serious engine damage.

The manual method of leaning cannot be employed in aircraft with fuel injected engines because a fuel injection system distributes the fuel more evenly to each cylinder, and the rough running would be less apparent. Attempting to lean the mixture to the onset of roughness could result in the mixture control being pulled back to the idle cut-off position, starving the engine of fuel and stopping it. Again, this would drastically reduce your aircraft's range and endurance!

The mixture can also be adjusted to produce maximum power prior to take-off from a hot and high airfield. After running up the engine to full throttle (take care that the aircraft doesn't creep forward against the brakes), lean the mixture setting until the engine rpm reading peaks at best power. When this occurs, note the position of the mixture control and quickly return it to the fully rich position. The engine should continue to run smoothly without any surge in power. Continued smooth running indicates that the selected mixture setting was correct, and the control can be readjusted to that setting. It will then be set at the best power position ready for take-off. It is preferable to lean the mixture early in the take-off run,

A Boeing 737 ('baby Boeing') receives underwing refuelling. The 737 is the most numerous of jet airliners to be built, outnumbering the popular Boeing 727. Its first flight was in 1967, and it is still in production today, proving its worth as an economical short-haul airliner.

provided this does not distract you from controlling the aircraft correctly. Otherwise, lean the mixture immediately prior to entering the runway for take-off. This method also is suitable for aircraft equipped with constant-speed propellers. In this case, during a full-power run-up, the propeller will be at the fine-pitch stop and will stay there until the take-off is well under way before moving toward a coarse setting. Therefore, the constant-speed unit will not mask the increase in engine rpm when leaning the mixture to the best power setting.

If your aircraft is equipped with a carburettor air temperature gauge, it can be employed to good advantage when leaning the mixture. The engine will produce more power when cold air is flowing through the carburettor because this will have a greater density than warm air. However, the fuel will not vaporize so readily if the air is cold; the optimum temperature for carburettor inlet air lies in the range of 30–35°C (90–100°F). By applying a small amount of carburettor heat, the temperature can be increased to the desired range for improved vaporization. That said, caution is required to prevent the cylinder head or exhaust gas temperatures from exceeding their specified limits.

Some pilots claim that the use of carburettor heat is 'all or nothing'. Nevertheless, it is a variable control and, if used with caution and in conjunction with a carburettor air temperature gauge, it can regulate the carburettor air temperature as required.

Fuel Flow Gauge

On engines equipped with carburettors, the fuel pressure gauge indicates the fuel pressure supplied by the fuel pump to the carburettor. Fuel is delivered by the pump at a constant pressure in the range 0.35–6.3kg/sq.cm (0.5–9lb/sq.in), and remains virtually constant for all power settings. Changing the power setting or operating the mixture control has no effect on the fuel pressure.

On a fuel injected engine, however, the fuel pressure is variable. In a fuel injection system, fuel is supplied under pressure to the fuel control unit. The fuel pressure required by the engine in various phases of flight (take-off, climb, cruise, etc) is determined by engine power and selected by the use of the mixture control. The required fuel flow for each phase of flight may be marked on the fuel flow gauge, or it can be found in the POH or on an instrument panel placard. Adjusting the mixture control will change the rate of flow, which in turn affects the fuel/air ratio.

The fuel flow gauge is connected to the fuel line between the system's fuel metering unit and fuel injectors. With this arrangement, the fuel pressure and fuel flow can be indicated as variable quantities on the gauge and used for leaning purposes. A fuel injected engine generally operates with a higher fuel pressure than an engine equipped with a carburettor. For example, the Continental IO-520-F engine operates at a fuel pressure of 2.5–13.7kg/sq.cm (3.5–19.5lb/sq.in) and has a corresponding fuel flow figure of 26–64ltr/hr (6–14imp.gal/hr or 7–17USgal/hr).

The Cylinder Head Temperature Gauge

The preferred instrument for monitoring the leaning operation is the EGT gauge. In its absence, however, the CHT gauge may be used to adjust the mixture to the best economy setting. Lean to peak CHT and watch for a decrease in temperature 25°C (77°F) below this value. This will indicate that the mixture is on the lean side of peak at the best economy setting. At peak CHT, the mixture will be set approximately half-way between best power and best economy. Although the CHT will peak near to peak EGT, the two will not coincide. The highest CHT readings coincide with the highest pressures in the cylinders, where the transfer of heat to the cylinder heads is at its greatest. Beyond this point, where the mixture is leaner, it burns longer and, therefore, the CHT is cooler. For maximum engine life, manufacturers recommend cruising at 125–150°C (257–302°F) on the rich of peak at 65–75 per cent brake horsepower. If you choose to run the engine on the lean side of peak, keep a careful eye on the CHT gauge, as this will lead to high exhaust valve temperatures that can shorten their life if operating above 65 per cent brake horsepower.

Be aware that setting best power cannot be done precisely by using the CHT gauge; an alternative method will have to be employed. Remember that the CHT reading should always remain around the middle of the green arc on the CHT gauge.

The Exhaust Gas Temperature Gauge

Most pilots consider the EGT gauge to be the best reference when leaning the mixture in light aircraft. The system incorporates a temperature probe that is positioned in the exhaust gas flow, preferably from the leanest cylinder, although this can vary with changes in power and altitude. At high power settings during the climb, the engine will run hotter. At the top of the climb, after levelling off, allow the EGT gauge reading to stabilize, since it will be affected by lag. Then lean the mixture setting slowly to avoid over-leaning. During the climb, lean to about 52°C (125°F) rich of peak to produce best power.

An improvement on the basic EGT gauge, which is connected to only one temperature sensing probe in the exhaust system, is the exhaust gas temperature analyser (EGTA). This has a temperature probe fitted in each cylinder's exhaust stack. A selector knob on the front of the instrument allows each cylinder to be checked in turn to ascertain the individual temperature readings. The highest temperature reading should be used as the reference for leaning.

Engine efficiency may be improved in some engines if they are run above peak EGT, between 10 and 38°C (50 and 100°F) on the lean side of peak, although some engines tend toward roughness around 18°C (25°F) lean of

Leaning Methods

The following table gives a brief summary of the different leaning techniques. Remember to follow the directions in the POH for allowable leaning limits for your aircraft.

Method	Best power (climb)	Economy (cruise)
Manual	Max rpm	Onset of roughness
Fuel flow gauge	As per flight manual	As per flight manual
CHT	Rich of peak CHT	25°C (77°F) lean of peak
EGT	52°C (125°F) rich side of peak	24°C (75°F) lean of peak
Exhaust gas analyser	As per flight manual	As per flight manual

peak. However, running on the rich side of peak ensures that the engine runs below peak temperature. This is easier on the engine and helps prolong its life, even though slightly more fuel is consumed. Again, follow the POH for your aircraft. Best economy is achieved at 10–38°C (50–100°F) on the lean side of peak, and best power at around 38°C (100°F) on the rich side of peak EGT.

The EGT gauge method of leaning relies on peak EGT occurring at the stoichiometric value. In other words, EGT is at its highest when all the fuel and air are burned completely. Above and below this value, burning will not be complete due to the mixture being too lean or too rich. This will cause temperatures that are slightly cooler than peak EGT.

The face of the EGT gauge may be marked in divisions rather than in degrees C or F, in which case, it is essential to identify the peak division for reference purposes.

CHAPTER 5
CARBURETTOR
ICING

Icing is the bane of all carburettors; it can occur at just about any time of day or year, even during nice sunny, summer weather. It can block the fuel flow through a carburettor and starve an engine of fuel. This has a bad effect on range and endurance!

All pilots are familiar with the term 'carburettor icing', but 'induction system icing' is a more appropriate description. For simplicity, however, I'll stick with the more familiar terminology in this chapter.

As student pilots, we were all taught by our flight instructors to apply carburettor heat before closing the throttle in flight, and to check it during our pre-flight engine run-up. I wonder how many pilots actually experienced carburettor icing during flight training. I know I never did, although I did encounter the condition a few months after gaining my PPL without recognizing it as such. I thought it was serious trouble when the engine started to run rough. I knew icing could cause engine roughness, but not to the extent I experienced on that flight. I quickly diverted to the nearest airport, only to be told that particles of ice ingested into the cylinders had caused the roughness. Plenty of other pilots have also been misled by the effects of icing.

A report issued by the American AOPA Air Safety Foundation states that in one six-year period in the USA, 193 aircraft accidents were caused by carburettor icing. A further 902 accidents during the same time span were accredited to engine failure from unknown causes. Some of these were probably the result of fuel mismanagement problems, as discussed previously. The statistics show that aircraft accidents attributed to carburettor icing occur during climb out after take-off, when icing is already present prior to take-off and during the cruise phase of flight when the throttle is partially closed. Does this mean that pilots are not using carburettor heat as often as they should? I believe so.

Carburettor icing is caused by various factors: changes in outside air temperature and humidity, evaporative cooling, throttle icing and impact induction icing. The result is that the venturi system becomes blocked by ice, preventing the fuel/air mixture from reaching the engine. This is followed by engine failure and termination of the flight.

TEMPERATURE/DEW POINT SPREAD

Taking relative humidity as a reference for determining the risk of icing can be an arbitrary method for most pilots, although I will include it as part of the discussion. A more practical and convenient reference point is the temperature/dew point spread, both figures being more readily available to pilots in met forecasts.

Checking the temperature/dew point spread prior to flight will give an indication of whether instrument or visual meteorological conditions (IMC or VMC) prevail – the closer the two figures, the greater the relative humidity. For example, when both figures are the same, they represent 100 per cent relative humidity and, therefore, very low cloud and below-IFR conditions. A forecast with a four-degree spread indicates low clouds and minimum VFR conditions; a two-degree spread points to minimum IFR conditions. A greater temperature spread is found on days with fewer or higher clouds.

TYPES OF CARBURETTOR ICING

So far, I have discussed carburettor icing in general. However, it can be classified into three main categories, depending on the method of formation. This doesn't mean that you are likely to experience one type of carburettor icing on one day, and a different type the next day. Any or all types of icing can be found at any one time, but they are all treated simply as carburettor icing. The three categories are fuel evaporative icing, throttle icing and impact induction icing.

Fuel Evaporative Icing

The most common form of icing experienced in aero engines is fuel evaporative icing. It can occur anywhere downstream of the point where fuel is mixed with the incoming air to the cylinders, particularly with float-type carburettors. The evaporation process accounts for 70 per cent of the total heat loss within the carburettor, cooling all the intake surfaces, which are wet with fuel, and also cooling the intake air, which may experience a temperature drop of up to 35°C (95°F). Moisture in the air turns to ice as it makes contact with the cold surfaces of the intake system. The important point to remember is that it is the water vapour present in the air that freezes, not the actual fuel; Avgas does not freeze at any normal temperature.

The outside air temperature (OAT) range at which fuel evaporative icing can be expected to form is between –10°C and +25°C (14°F and 76°F). Icing is very unlikely at temperatures above 25°C (76°F), no matter what the relative humidity. Below –10°C (14°F), icing is also unlikely, unless any supercooled water droplets are present. If the ambient relative humidity is below 60 per cent, regardless of temperature, icing should not be expected. On the other hand, fuel evaporative icing will occur readily at ambient

The Consolidated PBY Catalina long-range, maritime patrol flying boat was first built in 1935. It has a cruise speed of 95–155kt (110–180mph) and a range of 2,200n.miles (2,500st.miles).

temperatures of around 13°C (55°F). The degree of evaporative cooling depends on the fuel/air ratio, manifold pressure, inlet air temperature and humidity, and the volatility of the fuel. The degree to which each factor affects carburettor icing is a complex variable. So, what is fuel evaporative cooling? A simple example is to lick the back of your hand and gently blow on it. Feel the coolness? That's evaporative cooling.

Throttle Icing

It is usual for throttle icing to occur when the throttle is closed to reduce power, or when the engine is idling. With the throttle butterfly valve almost closed, the speed of the intake air is increased as it tries to rush through the narrowing gap between the butterfly and carburettor walls. This causes a reduction in air pressure and also a drop in temperature of the fuel/air mixture (remember Bernoulli's principle). Water vapour in the air condenses and ice is formed around the butterfly valve. To counter this, I have my own rule of thumb, which is to apply carburettor heat prior to reducing power below 2,000rpm at any time.

This type of carburettor icing can form with an OAT of up to 5°C (41°F). Consequently, it is important to check for carburettor icing prior to beginning the take-off run when the temperature is around 5°C (41°F).

Opening the throttle helps to clear any ice to a certain degree, the restriction between the butterfly valve and the carburettor walls being reduced as the throttle is opened, which has the opposite effect to closing the throttle.

Impact Induction Icing

This type of icing can be a problem for any kind of piston engine, regardless of whether it is fuel injected or carbureted. Moreover, turbo-prop engines can also become victims to this type of icing.

Impact induction icing is similar to airframe glaze icing, in that it forms under the same atmospheric conditions. If airframe icing is present, there is a strong possibility that impact induction icing will be present too. Aircraft flown under IFR are more prone to this type of icing when flying through wet snow, clouds or freezing rain with large, supercooled water droplets present and a relatively high ambient air temperature between –10°C and 0°C (14°F and 32°F). However, the worst possible condition for glaze icing is just below the freezing point, especially at high cruise speeds, when the ice is wet, porous and freezes readily. At lower temperatures, the ice becomes drier and is less likely to adhere to the airframe.

Supercooled water droplets in air temperatures below freezing strike the engine's intake system and form ice on the intake screens, scoop, butterfly valve and other protrusions in the intake system. The intake air to the carburettor is restricted by the ice build-up on forward facing parts of the intake system. This upsets the fuel metering system, enriches the fuel/air mixture and causes rough engine running, which may lead to engine failure. In this situation, the alternate air intake system, either manual or automatic, should be activated to prevent engine stoppage. Alternate air is similar to carburettor heat, but it is essential to lean the mixture when using it.

PRE-TAKE-OFF CHECK

Carburettor heat should be applied during engine run-up as a check to ensure that it is working – you should observe a drop of about 100rpm on the engine tachometer. Several minutes may elapse between making the check and starting the take-off run, time enough for carburettor icing to form if the atmospheric conditions are conducive. Such conditions can be expected when the ambient air temperature is 20°C (68°F) or below, combined with a relative humidity of over 50 per cent. In this situation, check the carburettor heat again prior to take-off. However, never use it during the actual take-off run.

When carburettor heat is applied, the warm air entering the engine's cylinders is less dense, reducing the amount of oxygen in the fuel/air mixture. This causes a drop in the maximum power available of around 2 per cent brake horsepower for every 10°C (50°F) rise in intake air temperature, or about 15 per cent brake horsepower total. Detonation could also be a problem, hence the need to check for carburettor icing before take-off.

The use of carburettor heat should also be avoided during the climb at any time with power settings above 75 per cent brake horsepower. Below this figure, carburettor heat can be left on continuously if needed. However, because hot air is less dense than cold air, the mixture will need leaning to prevent rough engine running, whether ice is present or not.

THE CARBURETTOR HEAT SYSTEM

When carburettor heat is selected, the knob or lever opens a valve to direct hot air into the intake system through the air mixture unit. The hot air is obtained from the same source as cabin hot air, from an air scoop located near the engine exhaust system.

Immediately after start-up, an idling engine will not provide very much heat, and with the throttle butterfly closed, it will take only a small amount of ice to block it. This is why a check for icing must be made prior to take-off, as described previously. During a prolonged glide, open the throttle every 1,000ft or so in the descent to keep the engine warm enough to provide heat. A word or warning, however: don't use carburettor heat for long periods on the ground. The usual filtered air intake is bypassed, allowing unfiltered air to enter the engine, along with grass, dust, etc, which causes undue wear to the pistons and cylinder walls.

An indication of icing on an aircraft with a fixed-pitch propeller is a gradual decrease in airspeed and engine rpm, followed by the engine running rough. If a constant-speed propeller is installed, the constant-speed unit governor maintains a constant rpm, while the airspeed and manifold pressure reduce.

Applying carburettor heat when ice is present will cause the engine to run rough initially, quite severely in some instances, as the ice is melted and ingested into the cylinders, and also by the over-rich mixture. The rpm will drop briefly; the engine may even stop if the icing is really bad. During one of my experiences of carburettor icing, the rpm dropped down to around 1,800–2,000rpm on an aircraft with a fixed-pitch propeller. Normally, a drop in rpm is to be expected, followed by a rise to a engine speed slightly higher than before carburettor heat was applied. Turning off the heat will produce an even higher rpm – by about 50–100rpm – as cold denser air freely returns to the cylinders. The drop in rpm or manifold pressure is caused by the venturi being restricted by ice. After the ice has melted, the venturi is clear and allows a normal airflow. As a result, the rpm and manifold pressure return to the original setting. If the icing is extreme, apply full power and, if possible, climb at a low forward speed, which will reduce engine cooling to make more heat. The extra heat produced by the engine at full power will help cure the icing problem.

If icing is present and you delay applying carburettor heat, the ice can build to a point where it suffocates the engine, causing it to stop. With the engine no longer running, there may not be sufficient heat available from the exhaust for long enough to melt the ice, making a restart impossible. This is quite often the cause of engine failures that lead to forced landings. After the aircraft has been on the ground for a while, the ice melts and the engine can be restarted, leaving no apparent cause for the failure. All that was required was a dose of carburettor heat at the appropriate time. Therefore, check for icing frequently.

CARBURETTOR AIR TEMPERATURE GAUGE

Some aircraft have a carburettor air temperature gauge, which is marked with the temperature range where icing is likely to form. The use of partial, but sufficient, carburettor heat to keep the carburettor air temperature out of this range should ensure freedom from icing problems. If an aircraft does not have such a gauge, partial heat should not be used. Apply full carburettor heat to check for and clear any carburettor ice that may be present. If the ambient air temperature is just below the icing level (−10°C/14°F), applying carburettor heat can raise the temperature into the range where icing will occur. In effect, this causes icing instead of prevents it.

CHAPTER 6
FLIGHT PLAN FUEL

Flight planning is a very important aspect of operating any aircraft. Determining the quantity of fuel required for a trip and ensuring that the correct amount of fuel is loaded are the responsibility of the pilot-in-command. To this end, pilots of large, multi-engine transport aircraft are provided with comprehensive graphs and tables for calculating aircraft performance and fuel requirements for each phase of a flight.

Light aircraft pilots have only limited information provided in the aircraft pilot's operating handbook (POH), reflecting the lower aircraft weight and lower volume of fuel carried by such aircraft. This usually takes the form of simple tables of true airspeed (TAS), power, fuel consumption, and range and endurance for a few selected altitudes. The TAS, power and fuel consumption figures are good, but the range and endurance figures should be ignored completely for flight planning purposes because they are only of academic interest. They normally show the total range and endurance, assuming the aircraft starts and ends its run at the given altitude, with the mixture leaned and in no-wind, ISA conditions. Such a situation is rarely encountered in practice, especially over the wide area that would be covered on a typical cross-country flight. Fuel allowance for taxiing, take-off and climb out may or may not be included in these figures (although this could be provided as a separate table).

Aircraft performance charts are based on correct use of the mixture control. A setting of fully rich burns more fuel, so the true range and endurance will be somewhat less than the book figures. In fact, we are more interested in endurance, not range. It is the available fuel that keeps the aircraft airborne for a given length of time (endurance). The range is determined by other variable factors, such as TAS, wind velocity, temperature and altitude.

When training for our Private Pilot Licences, cross-country flights were of a relatively short distance. We filled the aircraft's tanks with about four hours' worth of fuel for a flight lasting about two hours or so. In a two-seat basic trainer of 100–150bhp, the amount of fuel used during taxiing, take-off and climb out was of little concern to us. However, as we progress to flying greater distances in aircraft of higher performance, this fuel must be taken into consideration.

So, how much fuel should be allowed for cruising from the total amount in the tanks? The following is a breakdown of the fuel required for various phases of flight. Every flight will require sufficient fuel to cover all the phases listed, known as 'trip fuel'. Civil aviation regulations, aero club rules, company policy or plain common sense may dictate the requirements of additional fuel given under 'reserve fuel'.

The fuel needed for different stages of a flight can be classified under the following headings:

Trip Fuel
- Start-up, taxi and take-off.
- Climb.
- Cruise.
- Descent.
- Approach and landing.

Reserve Fuel
- General reserves.
- Overshoot.
- Diversion.
- Approach and landing at alternate.
- Holding.
- Contingency reserve percentage.

The Grumman AA-5 Cheetah/Traveller appeared in 1971. Its all-up weight of 1,000kg (2,200lb) is equivalent to the allowable taxi fuel of a Boeing 747B.

TRIP AND RESERVE FUEL

The trip fuel is the fuel allowed, and expected to be used, for a flight from one point to another. The reserve fuel is additional fuel carried on board to cover any unexpected contingencies, such as an overshoot or missed approach, or a diversion to an alternate airfield.

Start-Up and Taxi Fuel

Every type of aircraft has a maximum take-off weight (MTOW). Some aircraft are designed to carry extra fuel for taxiing to the take-off position, over and above the maximum all-up weight (MAUW). It must be remembered that the MTOW still applies in such cases, which means that all the extra fuel loaded on board for taxiing must be consumed before the take-off begins. The take-off weight (TOW) plus taxi fuel is known as the ramp weight. The fuel flow required for taxiing a light aircraft is around 25 per cent of the cruise fuel flow, or about 7kg/hr (15lb/hr) of fuel. Taxi time only lasts

The Fokker Dr1 Triplane is a surprisingly small aircraft for a fighter. It is notable for being the mount of the famous German ace Baron Manfred von Richtofen. It had a short endurance time of 1hr 30min.

around 5–10min, so actual fuel used is minimal when compared to a Boeing 747-200B for example, which can burn up to 1,000kg (2,200lb) of fuel for taxiing – equivalent to the MAUW of a Grumman Cheetah! As you can see, taxi fuel can be a significant factor for pilots of large aircraft, and although the amount of fuel required to taxi a light aircraft is relatively small, it should be borne in mind. This is particularly important if the aircraft is used for several short flights before being refuelled. In a flight training establishment or when making short commuter runs, the time spent taxiing is relatively greater than it would be for one long flight before refuelling.

Climb Fuel

Naturally, fuel flow during the climb will be greater than in the cruise. One rule of thumb is to add 2ltr (0.4imp.gal/0.5USgal) of fuel per cylinder to the cruise fuel flow to find the approximate fuel consumption rate during the climb. For a four-cylinder engine burning 30ltr (7imp.gal/8USgal) of fuel per hour during the cruise, allow 40ltr (9imp.gal/10USgal) per hour for the duration of the climb. This method works fine for basic two- and four-seat light aircraft with fixed-pitch propellers. Moving up to higher-performance singles or light twins with more powerful engines, however, is a different matter, and the POH should be consulted for the exact amount of fuel required. A good POH will provide a table of fuel required during engine start-up, taxi, take-off and climb to given altitudes. Then it is a simple matter to add on the cruise and reserve fuels when working out the fuel required.

Cruise Fuel

The figures for range and endurance given in the POH will be based on flying with the mixture leaned to best economy, or peak cylinder head temperature (CHT) or peak exhaust gas temperature (EGT). This will produce a fuel saving of approximately 15 per cent. It follows that if the mixture is left at the fully rich setting for the cruise, the true range will be less than that quoted in the POH. The cruise fuel flow for a basic light aircraft will be a fairly constant figure. It is normal practice to commit to memory the fuel consumption and TAS for the light aircraft that we fly regularly. Once again, however, moving up to bigger and heavier aircraft will require reference to the POH for the exact figures for fuel consumption and TAS. These can vary with weight, ambient temperature, cruise altitude, power settings and leaning techniques. All of these factors can have a great influence on range and endurance.

Descent Fuel

Not surprisingly, during the descent, fuel flow will be less than in the cruise, but only by a small amount. Consequently, it is common practice to plan descent fuel at the normal cruise fuel flow rate. Using this method of calculation will ensure that a small amount of fuel will remain in the tanks – erring on the safe side.

Approach and Landing Allowance
This is insignificant for pilots of light aircraft, but not so for those who fly heavier aircraft.

Reserve Fuel
Civil aviation regulations require that a reserve fuel allowance be added to the flight plan fuel to cover any extension of flight time greater than that planned. The amount of fuel held in reserve should be calculated at the cruise fuel flow for at least thirty minutes, but allowing a one-hour reserve is a more sensible move.

The importance of reserve fuel cannot be overemphasized. Numerous problems can crop up during a flight, each sufficient to keep you in the air for longer than planned. Reserve fuel is there for such unexpected setbacks, such as a diversion, holding, a go-around, increasing headwind, getting lost (bad navigation) or losing an engine on a multi-engine aircraft.

Reserve fuel is akin to life insurance. For 99 per cent of your flying career, you won't need that reserve fuel – until the day a flight doesn't go according to plan. Then, if there is insufficient or no reserve fuel in the tanks, you will be wishing you had some – along with life insurance!

Diversion
A diversion en route may be required for a variety of reasons, such as air traffic, low fuel, a mechanical problem or adverse weather. If an instrument approach is made at the destination airport, followed by a missed approach, a diversion to an alternate may follow. This will entail the usual climb out, cruise, descent and approach, for which the relevant amount of fuel must be available. Always make sure you have enough fuel on board to accommodate any diversion.

Holding
In congested airspace, a holding-pattern procedure or an orbit if VFR may be requested by air traffic control at any time. Again, fuel will be required to cover this eventuality. Although this would be negligible for a light aircraft, it would be significant for a larger one and must be included in the flight plan. Typically, this would be sufficient to allow around thirty minutes' flight at normal cruise speed.

Contingency Reserve Percentage
In addition to carrying the legally required reserve fuel, it may be prudent to add a contingency reserve percentage. This is to allow for any discrepancies encountered due to the engine using more fuel than normal, or errors in instrumentation, etc. It is the pilot's responsibility to determine the amount of reserve fuel to be carried in the aircraft, generally with flying club or company operating policy as a guide. If you own the aircraft, the decision will be placed on your shoulders alone.

Legal Fuel Reserves

As an example, New Zealand civil aviation regulations require the following fuel reserves to be carried:

- For all fixed-wing aircraft on VFR operations by day – thirty minutes; by night – forty-five minutes.
- Helicopter operations – twenty minutes.
- Non-turbine powered, IFR, fixed-wing operations – sufficient fuel to divert to a suitable alternate aerodrome (if so required), plus forty-five minutes at holding consumption rate at 1,500ft.
- All turbine powered, fixed-wing aircraft and helicopter IFR operations – sufficient fuel to divert to a suitable alternate aerodrome (if so required), plus thirty minutes at holding consumption rate at 1,500ft.

Remember that these are the legal minimums set by law. Aero club or company policy may require greater reserves to be carried. If you are down to these minimum requirements and still flying, there will be very little fuel remaining in the tanks. Good airmanship dictates that you use higher minimum reserves for your own protection and peace of mind.

Therefore, carefully consider all contingencies before deciding on how much reserve fuel to carry. Will thirty minutes be sufficient, or should the reserve be extended to an hour or more? When airborne, do not be tempted to extend your flight time by using reserve fuel to get to your destination. Good airmanship will dictate a landing for refuelling before continuing the flight. Reserve fuel is there to cover the unexpected; stretching your range by using that reserve is not acceptable and demonstrates very poor decision making. Remember that reserve fuel is your life insurance!

FUEL MEASUREMENT

Many countries measure fuel in metric litres; others prefer imperial gallons or US gallons. The fuel tanks and gauges in aircraft may be calibrated in any of these units, but aircraft load sheets may need to be completed using different units to the fuel-gauge calibrations, depending on the system favoured by the fuel supplier. This can lead to confusion when converting from one system to another, and to the wrong amounts of fuel being loaded aboard. As a result, many pilots have discovered in flight that their aircraft doesn't have the range and endurance they initially calculated, and they have ended up short of their destination. Therefore, make sure you use the correct units and conversion factors when planning your fuel supply. Whenever possible, employ only one system of units to avoid having to convert your calculations (*see* Fuel Calculation Formulas).

The ultimate in long-range, jet transport aircraft, the Boeing 777. This is the standard -200 model. The -200 LR (long-range) version can fly up to 9,400n.miles (10,800st.miles) without refuelling. Planning the fuel requirements for a flight is of major concern with aircraft of this size.

FUEL LOG

When flying, keep a fuel log in addition to your navigation log. Include the fuel required for the various phases of flight and the total amount available. Record the time of each tank change to help keep the fuel load balanced, and so that you know where and how much fuel remains. Monitor the fuel gauges and compare the readings with the log to confirm fuel remaining. Calculate the fuel-stop ground speed and enter it in the log (*see* Fuel Calculation Formulas). If your ground speed falls to this figure, it will warn you that you are about to use your reserve fuel unless you land to refuel. An alternate method is to calculate the time to land, based on the safe endurance for the fuel available. Whatever method you use, the fuel log will help you keep track of the fuel situation for the flight and avoid fuel shortage problems.

CRUISE CONTROL METHODS

The choice of cruise control method is an important part of your pre-flight planning. Several different methods are available to the air transport pilot, but the light aircraft pilot only has the choice of using constant power (the most common method) or constant airspeed.

The change in aircraft weight due to fuel burn-off is very slight in light aircraft, but it is of great significance for larger aircraft flying long routes. A Piper Cherokee, for example, loses weight at the rate of approximately 270kg/hr (60lb/hr) due to fuel burn, not a great amount when compared to a heavy transport. In fact, about 15 per cent of a Cessna 172's all-up weight consists of fuel, compared to 22 per cent for a Douglas DC-3 and 40 per cent for a Boeing 747.

As the weight decreases, however, the aircraft will tend to climb unless the angle of attack is reduced. This, of course, will lead to an increase in airspeed, requiring a reduction in power setting. Thus, the pilot has the choice of flying at constant power and a steadily increasing speed, or at constant speed with the need to steadily reduce power.

Constant Power

As mentioned, constant power is the most common cruise control method used by pilots of light aircraft. It is the best bet, because the aircraft weight does not vary by any appreciable amount during flight. The power can be adjusted to the required setting and left there for the entire cruise portion of the trip. We accept whatever true airspeed results from this power setting, making engine handling, pre-flight fuel planning and in-flight fuel handling easier. The only disadvantage is the slight increase in TAS as the weight decreases with fuel burn-off. Nevertheless, for the route lengths flown by the average light aircraft, this speed increase can be ignored. However, it is an important factor for larger aircraft.

Constant Speed

Flight planning and navigation for larger aircraft are made simpler if TAS can be kept constant. However, this requires power reductions as the flight progresses. Careful choice of TAS will maintain optimum economy, and for this reason, air transport pilots normally employ constant-airspeed cruise control. Over very long routes, however, especially with turbine powered aircraft, increasing specific fuel consumption can negate its advantage. Transport pilots may also consider minimum-cost or long-range cruise control as other options.

FUEL CONSUMPTION

Throughout this book, the emphasis has been on the efficient use of fuel – how to get the most out of each litre, gallon, kilogram or pound of fuel. No matter how much you lean the mixture, the engine will still consume a given volume of fuel per hour in proportion to the brake horsepower being developed at the time. The rate of fuel consumed and the quantity of fuel on board determine the range and endurance of the aircraft in still-air conditions. Flying a given distance/range (R) at a given speed (V) will take a certain length of time (T) or endurance (R ÷ V = T). Endurance, in this case, refers to the time the aircraft can stay airborne on the given quantity of fuel at the given rate of fuel consumption. However, this is not the same as flying for endurance, where we use the minimum power required to stay airborne. More of this later (*see* Chapter 7).

Piston-engine and turbine-engine aircraft have their own definitions for fuel consumption. For a piston-engine aircraft, it is described as specific fuel consumption (SFC), which is proportional to the brake horsepower being developed at the time (*see* Figure 4, Chapter 4). The fuel consumption for a turbine aircraft is proportional to the thrust being developed, and is known as thrust specific fuel consumption (TSFC).

Specific fuel consumption is determined by the weight of fuel consumed per brake horsepower per hour. On average, this is 0.2kg (0.45lb)/bhp/hr for most light aircraft piston engines, and around 0.3kg (0.6lb)/bhp/hr for a turbine engine. The brake horsepower in the formula is that being developed at the chosen power setting at the time, not the rated maximum for the engine. Thus, it is obvious that selecting a lower power setting will reduce fuel consumption, because fuel consumption in pounds per hour equals specific fuel consumption multiplied by brake horsepower. By introducing TAS into the equation – (TAS ÷ SFC)×bhp – we find the aircraft's specific air range in air nautical miles per pound (anm/lb). The aircraft's total range in nautical miles is calculated by multiplying the total fuel weight by this specific air range figure. (*See* the section on E6-B computer formulas in Fuel Calculation Formulas for range and endurance calculations.) Substituting ground speed (G/S) for TAS gives us the ground range in ground nautical miles per pound (gnm/lb). This is of greater concern because it takes into account the wind velocity affecting the aircraft's ground speed.

Chapter 7
Aircraft
Performance

ASSOCIATED AERODYNAMICS

Flying for range and endurance involves many variables, and so far I have been looking at how fuel handling, leaning, fuel consumption, etc affect the task. In this chapter, I will examine the subject from an aerodynamic viewpoint, showing how this has an effect on the climb, cruise and descent portions of the trip, taking into consideration the range speed, optimum cruise speed and endurance speed. First, however, it will be worth reviewing these definitions:

- Range speed is defined as the least amount of fuel used per unit of distance (in nautical miles).
- Optimum cruise speed is defined as the least amount of fuel used per unit of velocity (in knots).
- Endurance speed is defined as the least amount of fuel used per unit of time (in minutes).

Note that the term 'the least amount of fuel' is mentioned in each definition. This is because using fuel efficiently is what flying for range and endurance is all about. Although we will be considering the aerodynamics of the aircraft in this chapter, that is the airframe's efficiency, the use of fuel still comes into the equation.

The power curves for a given aircraft can tell us a great deal about its performance characteristics. The power curves shown in Figure 5 have been plotted for sea-level conditions. The brake horsepower (BHP) line is affected by altitude, temperature, power settings and supercharging. It is a constant value for any given brake horsepower and will descend the graph at lower power settings and with increasing altitude. The thrust horsepower available curve (THP available) indicates the thrust delivered from the propeller, which varies with the true airspeed (TAS). The thrust horsepower available is always less than the brake horsepower because of losses in propeller efficiency. The propeller is designed to produce maximum efficiency at the aircraft's design cruise speed. Above and below that speed,

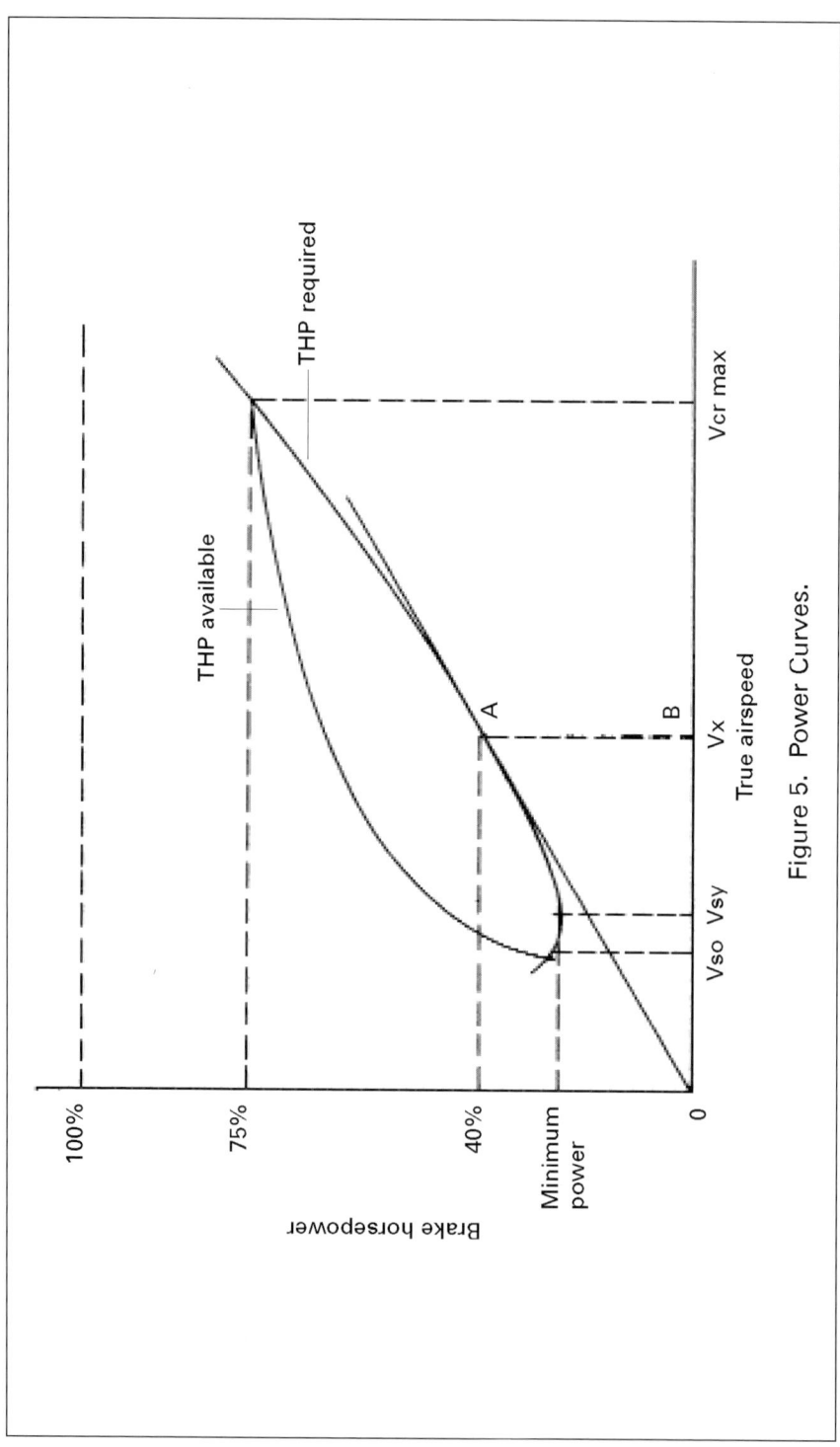

Figure 5. Power Curves.

its efficiency deteriorates, as indicated by the slope of the thrust horsepower available curve. The propeller efficiency and, hence, the thrust increases for the same brake horsepower, so the TAS will increase for any given brake horsepower. This results in the thrust horsepower available curve moving to the right in accordance with the greater speed. Most propellers have an efficiency factor of about 0.8–0.9. This means that the maximum thrust horsepower available is 80–90 per cent of the brake horsepower for any given TAS.

The lower thrust horsepower required (THP required) curve is related to the familiar drag curve, being calculated from the value of drag multiplied by velocity, but plotted for various true airspeeds. It is the same shape as the drag curve, but moved to the right in accordance with the increase in velocity. Remember that 'power required' is the minimum amount of power needed to maintain straight and level flight. Extra power is called for when climbing, turning and carrying out other manoeuvres, known as the excess thrust horsepower (ETHP).

Reference to Figure 5 is the starting point for determining the range speed. A tangent drawn from the origin '0' intersects the thrust horsepower required curve at point 'A'. From 'A', a horizontal line indicates the thrust horsepower required or percentage brake horsepower. A vertical line drawn down from 'A' gives the TAS range speed (Vy) at point 'B'. From this information, it is found:

$$\frac{AB}{OB} = \frac{Power}{TAS} = \frac{Drag \times TAS}{TAS} = minimum\ drag$$

In the foregoing formula, TAS cancels out, leaving drag. This is the minimum drag speed (Dmin). It is also shown on the graph as the drag/velocity ratio (D/V ratio). The reciprocal of this ratio is the maximum velocity/drag ratio (max V/D ratio), which is what concerns us. Another name for this is maximum lift/drag ratio (max L/D ratio), which occurs at a power setting of approximately 40 per cent brake horsepower. The speed also coincides with the maximum rate of climb (max RoC) speed and the best glide ratio, around 70–80kt for a typical light aircraft. At the lower power setting of 40 per cent brake horsepower, the first definition of range speed will be satisfied. That is 'the least amount of fuel used per unit of distance'. However, if we operated the engine at 40 per cent brake horsepower, the engine and propeller would not deliver their best efficiency, resulting in a loss in performance. Also, to cruise at 70kt is not aerodynamically efficient and defeats the purpose of using an aircraft for fast travel.

The range speed, or maximum lift/drag ratio speed, occurs at a value of around 1.5 Vso (flaps up, power off stall speed). From the speed for range, the fuel flow and air speed increases at a variable rate until eventually a certain speed is reached where the engine is burning the least extra fuel above optimum. This speed is known as the optimum cruise speed (V cruise), which is about a third greater than the range speed (V cruise = V range × 1.316). At the optimum cruise speed, the second definition is satisfied, namely that the engine is burning 'the least amount of fuel per unit of velocity'. The optimum cruise speed, being on the forward side of the power curve, ensures that the best fuel consumption – measured in ground nautical miles per gallon (gnm/g) – is achieved. The optimum cruise speed is achieved at 75 per cent brake horsepower and is normally referred to as the design cruise speed. We could say that the range speed and the optimum cruise speed correspond to the theoretical and practical cruise speeds.

THE EFFECTS OF ALTITUDE AND WEIGHT

For most light aircraft flying at maximum all-up weight (MAUW), it takes around 75 per cent brake horsepower to propel the aircraft at its design cruise speed. At lighter weights, the same speed can be achieved at 55–65 per cent brake horsepower. For a basic two-seat aircraft, this difference may not be noticeable due to the small variation in weight between a lightly loaded machine and its MAUW. Larger aircraft, with their greater weight range, however, require an appreciable difference in power settings to maintain cruise speed. Selecting the most favourable power setting for a flight requires careful flight planning and consideration of all the factors involved.

The curves for thrust horsepower available and thrust horsepower required at altitude are positioned differently on the graph from their sea-level counterparts (*see* Figure 6). The two curves move to the right because they are plotted for TAS and not indicated airspeed (IAS). The airspeed indicator is affected by the reduced air density at altitude, causing the IAS to be lower than TAS. If the power curves were plotted against IAS, they would move straight up the graph, but that is not so. Therefore, the thrust horsepower curves move up and to the right. At higher altitudes, where air density is reduced, less propeller thrust is available and the wings generate less lift. Therefore, a higher TAS is required to maintain the required lift. To provide a higher TAS, more power is called for, as indicated by the curve moving up and to the right.

The thrust horsepower available is also affected by increasing altitude, decreasing due to lower air density – less air is obtainable by the engine to produce power. The curve for thrust horsepower available descends the graph and moves to the right. With both curves moving toward each other, it can be seen that excess thrust horsepower (the difference between the two curves) decreases with increasing altitude, determining the surplus power in hand for climbing. Thus, the rate of climb decreases until, at the service ceiling, it has reduced to 100ft/min, dropping further to zero rate of climb at the absolute ceiling.

From the curve for thrust horsepower required, it can be seen that the range speed (Vy) increases with altitude. If the aircraft weight is below that

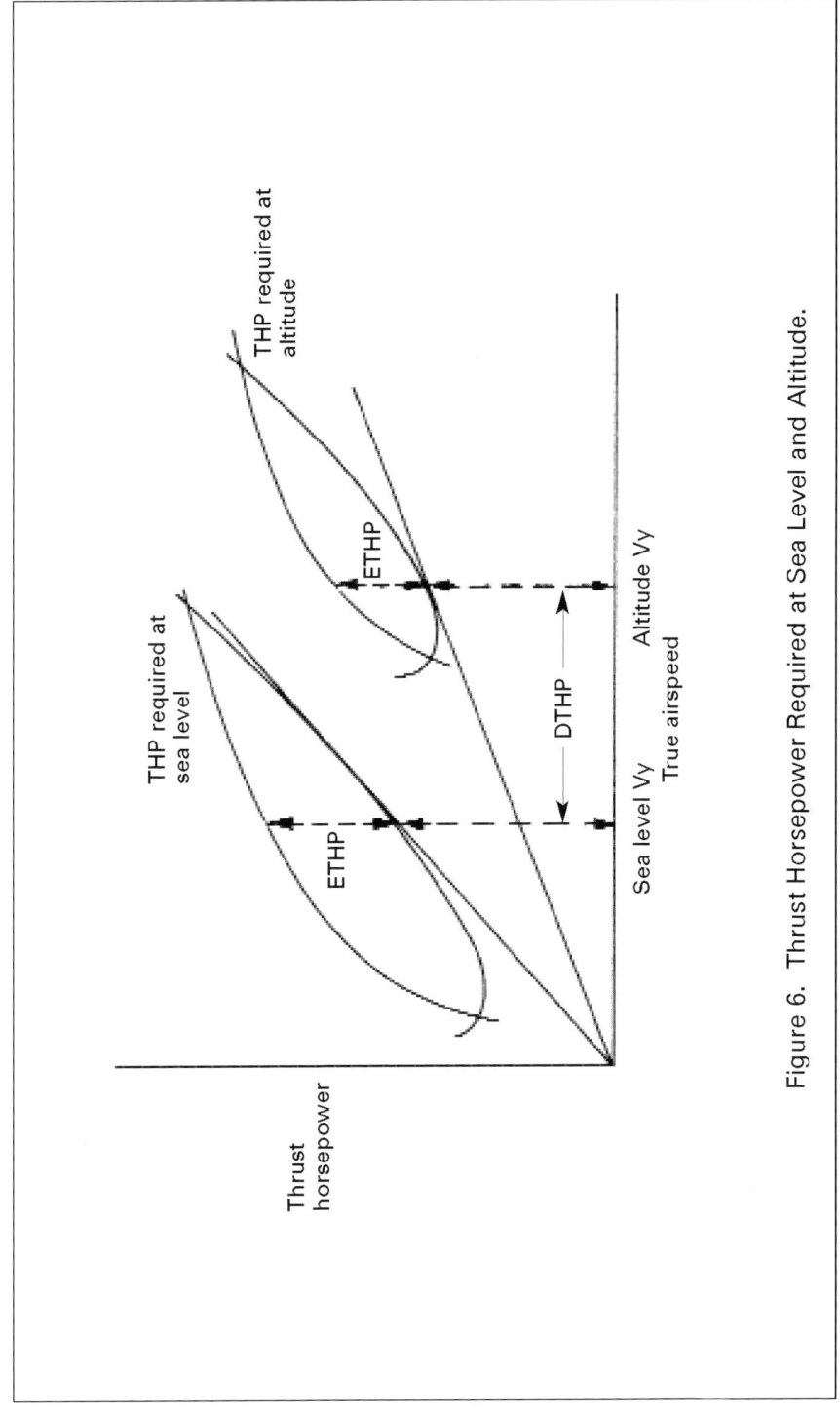

Figure 6. Thrust Horsepower Required at Sea Level and Altitude.

of the MAUW during the climb, thrust horsepower required is less, as indicated on the graph by being lower than the curve for MAUW. Therefore, greater ETHP is available at lighter weights, resulting in greater rates of climb. The effect of rising altitude is to cause the power required to increase, and the power available to decrease, resulting in reduced climb performance, but improved cruise performance. So at what altitude should the aircraft be flown to achieve the maximum range? This depends on three factors: airframe, IAS/TAS ratio, and engine and propeller.

The Airframe
A wing's maximum lift/drag ratio (max L/D) will be achieved at the same angle of attack at any altitude, regardless of aircraft weight. The IAS will also remain constant at all altitudes for a given angle of attack. However, an increase in aircraft weight will require an increase in IAS to maintain a constant lift/drag ratio. A higher airspeed calls for more power from the engine. In turn, the engine needs more fuel to produce more power, but more fuel equates to greater weight, and so the cycle continues. Greater weight requires more lift, and the higher IAS produces more drag in proportion. The result is a proportionate loss in range. Conversely, a reduction in weight will provide an increase in range. Maintaining a constant IAS will result in the same amount of drag at all altitudes. Therefore, as far as the airframe is concerned, range will be the same at any altitude, and will increase or decrease only with a change in aircraft weight.

The IAS/TAS Ratio
At a constant power setting, the TAS will increase with altitude for a constant IAS at the rate of approximately 1kt/1,000ft, as shown in Figure 7. Because the IAS is lower than the TAS, and therefore closer to the best range speed, the requirement for the first definition will be achieved, 'the least amount of fuel used per unit of distance'. The higher TAS for the same fuel flow at the optimum cruise speed will satisfy the requirement of the second definition, 'the least amount of fuel used per unit of velocity'. By flying higher, the TAS increases for a given IAS or, in other words, the IAS/TAS ratio improves with altitude. Therefore, where the IAS/TAS ratio is concerned, flying at higher altitudes is the requirement.

The Engine and Propeller
We must also take into consideration the engine and propeller when studying flying for range. For the engine and propeller to operate at their maximum efficiency, the best altitude will be at the full-throttle height. This is around 7,000–8,000ft at 75 per cent brake horsepower for a normally aspirated (carburettor equipped) engine, and considerably higher if the engine is turbocharged. Both full-throttle height and range will increase with a decrease in power setting. Figure 7 shows that at a power setting of 75 per cent brake horsepower, the TAS will increase from 133kt at 2,500ft

The Corby Starlet is an economical single-seat homebuilt aircraft. Engines up to 80bhp can be used, while fuel tanks can hold 53ltr (12imp.gal/14USgal) with no reserves, giving an endurance of approximately 3hr 45min and a range of around 440n.miles (500st.miles).

to 137kt at 6,500ft. This is an increase of 1kt/1,000ft. Power then drops from 75 per cent brake horsepower at the full-throttle height of around 7,500ft to 65 per cent brake horsepower at about 10,000ft, and continues to decrease with altitude. At 65 per cent brake horsepower, TAS rises from 124kt at 2,500ft to 132kt at 10,000ft. Range also increases with altitude and lower power settings, from 660n.miles at 2,500 feet to 680n.miles at 6,500 feet, using 75 per cent brake horsepower. There is a further increase to 730n.miles with a reduced power setting of 65 per cent brake horsepower at 6,500ft. Cruising at 10,000 feet at 65 per cent brake horsepower stretches the range to 746n.miles.

To return to the question about the optimum altitude to achieve maximum range, as we have seen, the airframe is happy to cruise at any altitude where the constant IAS produces the same range. However, the IAS/TAS ratio improves with altitude, and the engine and propeller operate more efficiently at the engine's full-throttle height. Therefore, the best altitude to fly will be at the full-throttle height for the power setting chosen. Your choice of power setting and altitude will have a direct bearing on the range of your aircraft. Become familiar with the pilot's operating handbook (POH) for your aircraft, bearing in mind that the range figures given indicate

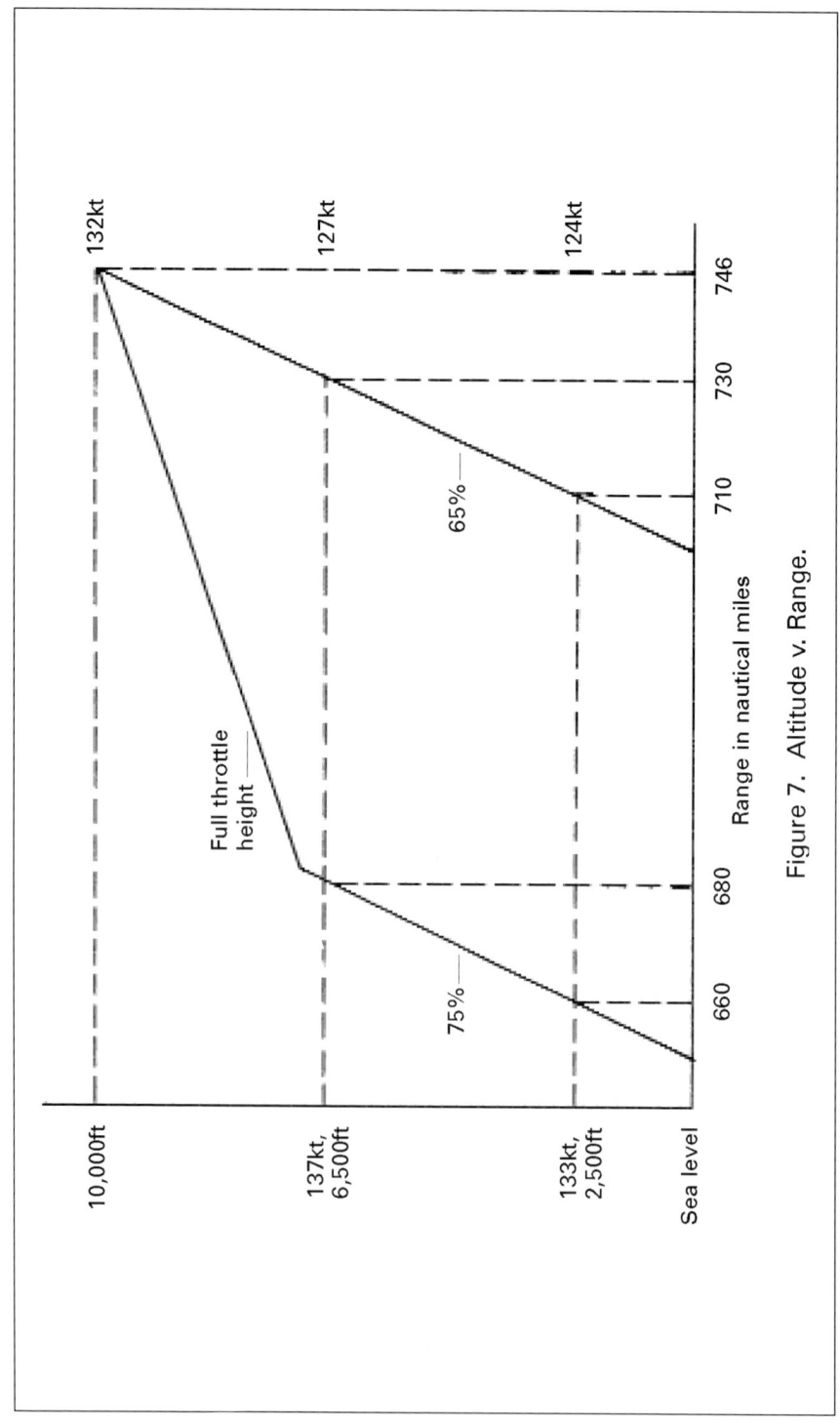

Figure 7. Altitude v. Range.

'book range'; they may or may not include fuel for taxiing, climbing, etc. The numbers used in Figure 7 are taken from the Cesssna 207 handbook. They are used to indicate the distance the aircraft would travel under no-wind conditions at a given altitude, airspeed, fuel flow and fuel quantity. They do not take into consideration the fuel required for taxiing, take-off, climb out, descent, approach, reserve. etc. However, a separate table does exist for climb-fuel calculations. Therefore, the true range would be somewhat less than that indicated in the POH. Nevertheless, the figures shown in Figure 7 are indicative of how range and true airspeed vary with percentage brake horsepower and altitude.

In conclusion, the best altitude for range flying depends on the airframe, the IAS/TAS ratio, and the engine/propeller combination. To recapitulate, and taking each factor in turn:

1. The airframe will cruise efficiently at any altitude at a given angle of attack and given IAS.
2. The IAS/TAS ratio improves with higher altitude.
3. The engine and propeller are most efficient at the full-throttle height.

Therefore, whenever possible, choose the full-throttle height or higher to achieve maximum range. Don't forget, however, that the wind velocity usually increases with altitude, affecting the aircraft's range by either increasing or decreasing it. Consequently, wind velocity must always be taken into consideration.

WIND EFFECT ON RANGE

So far, we have only considered range when unaffected by wind velocity, that is the still-air range (SAR). We will now look at some examples of the wind's effect on range, calculated on the E6-B air navigation computer, comparing two aircraft with different cruise speeds. Let's assume one aircraft cruises at 135kt, and the other at 110kt, with a headwind component of 20kt outbound and, of course, a tailwind component of 20kt when on the home leg. A headwind component is considered negative, being subtracted from the TAS to find the ground speed (G/S). Conversely, a tailwind component is positive.

Consider a round-trip flight of 800n.miles, that is 400n.miles out and 400n.miles back home. The faster aircraft with the 135kt cruise speed would complete the total distance in 5hr 56min in no-wind conditions. Now factor in the 20kt wind component. This produces a G/S of 115kt on the outbound leg, giving a time of 3hr 29min to cover the 400n.miles, which is 31min longer than the no-wind time. The return leg, at a G/S of 155kt, will be flown in 2hr 35min – a gain of 23min over the still-air time. Notice the effect that the wind has on time: 31min extra with a headwind component, and 23min less with a tailwind component. (A 20kt wind is relatively weak

Developed from the Fletcher FU-24 series of agricultural aircraft, the PAC Cresco 750 sports a Pratt & Whitney PT6-A turbo-prop engine of 750shp. The result is a cruise speed of 140kt (160mph) with a range of 364n.miles (420st.miles) and an endurance of three hours. Turbo-prop engines are uneconomical at low altitude where ag aircraft operate, but the increase in engine power is the main attraction.

compared to what is normally encountered at altitude, but it serves our purpose in this particular instance.)

A headwind component has more effect than a tailwind component on the en-route time. When the aircraft is flying slower due to the former, the wind velocity has a longer time to affect the aircraft's progress. The sum of the times out and home gives a total flight time that is 8min longer than the no-wind time at the cruise speed of 135kt. The same 800n.miles round trip in the slower aircraft, cruising at 110kt, with the same wind, produces an outbound time of 4hr 28min, while the trip home takes 3hr 5min, a grand total of 7hr 33min. This is 17min longer than the time for a no-wind cruise at 110kt. As can be seen, the slower aircraft is affected more by the same wind velocity than the aircraft with the higher cruising speed. The slower the cruise speed, the greater the effect of wind velocity on range.

The 20kt headwind component is 18 per cent of the 110kt cruise speed, dropping to 15 per cent of the 135kt cruise speed. By comparing the percentage wind velocities, we can see that the higher percentage has a greater effect on range, proving the foregoing argument.

Another way to consider the effect of wind velocity is to compare the amount of fuel burned at different ground speeds in ground nautical miles per pound. (You could substitute statute miles or kilometres for nautical miles, and kilograms, litres, US gallons or imperial gallons for pounds in the formula. Always use the units that are familiar to you; I prefer to use nautical miles and pounds for fuel computations.) Flying at a cruise speed of 135kt, burning fuel at the rate of 90lb/hr, the consumption rate works out at 1.5gnm/lb. With 360lb of fuel available for cruising, the range will be 540n.miles in four hours. Using the same figures, but factoring in a 20kt headwind component for a ground speed of 115kt, gives a consumption of 1.27gnm/lb, while range is cut to 460n.miles (a 15 per cent reduction). A 20kt tailwind component added to the cruise speed, for a ground speed of 155kt, lowers consumption to 1.72gnm/lb with a 15 per cent jump in range to 620n.miles. Thus, both a headwind component and lower ground speed produce higher consumption and, therefore, less range. Conversely, a tailwind and higher ground speed give lower consumption and greater range.

(*See* Fuel Calculation Formulas for a method of determining fuel consumption in ground nautical miles per pound. By using this formula to calculate a variety of consumption figures for a selection of different forecast ground speeds, at various altitudes and fuel flows taken from your POH, you can find the best consumption figure. This will show the best altitude to use in respect of ground speed and fuel consumption to achieve maximum range, or the most fuel-efficient altitude to use in terms of fuel consumption.)

Some pilots claim that a lower power setting should be used when flying with a tailwind to save fuel, and a higher power setting when flying into a headwind. This argument is based on the fact that the TAS for maximum V/D ratio increases with a headwind and decreases with a tailwind. Therefore, flying against a headwind could benefit from an increase of power to raise the TAS. Taking an extreme example, if the TAS were the same as the headwind component, the ground speed would be zero. By increasing the TAS, some progress would be made against the wind. Similarly, decreasing the TAS and power for a tailwind will save fuel. The difference in speed for maximum V/D ratio in zero wind and a normal headwind component may only amount to 2–3kt in a light aircraft. It would not be worth adjusting the TAS to suit, unless you were attempting to save the maximum amount of fuel. Whenever you see a ground speed that is higher than the TAS on the DME or GPS, you are unlikely to be tempted to reduce power. Besides, the higher ground speed will get you to your destination quicker while achieving a lower fuel consumption, so you will be saving fuel.

A lack of wind, particularly over a large area, is a very rare occurrence; it is almost always present at varying velocities and must be taken into consideration when flying for range. Because wind velocity is always changing during a flight, a headwind component could increase, thus reducing range further. This could make it doubtful that you could reach your destination without an en-route fuel stop. One precaution you can take to guard against the effect of an increasing headwind is to calculate a minimum ground speed before take-off. If the ground speed decreases to this figure during the course of the flight, it will act as a reminder that the aircraft is reaching the limit of its range. At that point, it will be necessary to recalculate the distance to go versus fuel remaining; in other words, to decide whether there is sufficient fuel on board to continue the flight (*see* fuel-stop ground speed formula in Fuel Calculation Formulas).

STRETCHING THE RANGE

In the example given in Figure 9, flying at sea level increases total endurance by 30min. Reducing power from 75 per cent brake horsepower to 55 per cent brake horsepower increases endurance by 90min, based on a full tank. Because fuel consumption is proportional to brake horsepower being used, it follows that 20 per cent less fuel will be consumed. If you are getting low on fuel, increasing speed to get to an airport before the tanks run dry will not work. You will only increase your fuel consumption and decrease your range. Slowing down to endurance speed will save fuel and provide you with a better chance of reaching the airfield, albeit with a slow agonizing ride as you wait in suspense for the engine to quit! Having read this book, however, fuel mismanagement problems should not beset you. Use your fuel wisely, and fly safely and economically.

ENDURANCE FLYING

Unlike range flying, endurance flying is something you are not likely to do very often. Light aircraft pilots flying VFR may be called upon to orbit or hold near an airport while commercial traffic takes priority in take-off or landing. On the other hand, IFR pilots will be familiar with holding patterns associated with navigation aids. Whenever holding is called for, this is the time to reduce cruise speed to endurance speed.

The requirement of endurance flying is to use the least amount of fuel per unit of time. The emphasis is on time, as opposed to velocity, which is the case for range flying. Flying for range involves flying at the maximum L/D ratio, or D.min speed, as we have already seen. However, flying for endurance is achieved at the minimum power required speed. This is always less than the minimum drag speed, by almost a third. The speed itself is, of course, the TAS. At low altitudes, the TAS will be the same as, or close to, the IAS. This means that low altitude is desirable when flying for endurance (as shown in Figures 8 and 9), consistent with safety, ATC requirements, terrain clearance, etc.

Because induced drag increases with a decrease in speed, the drag will be slightly greater at the endurance speed than at the minimum drag speed

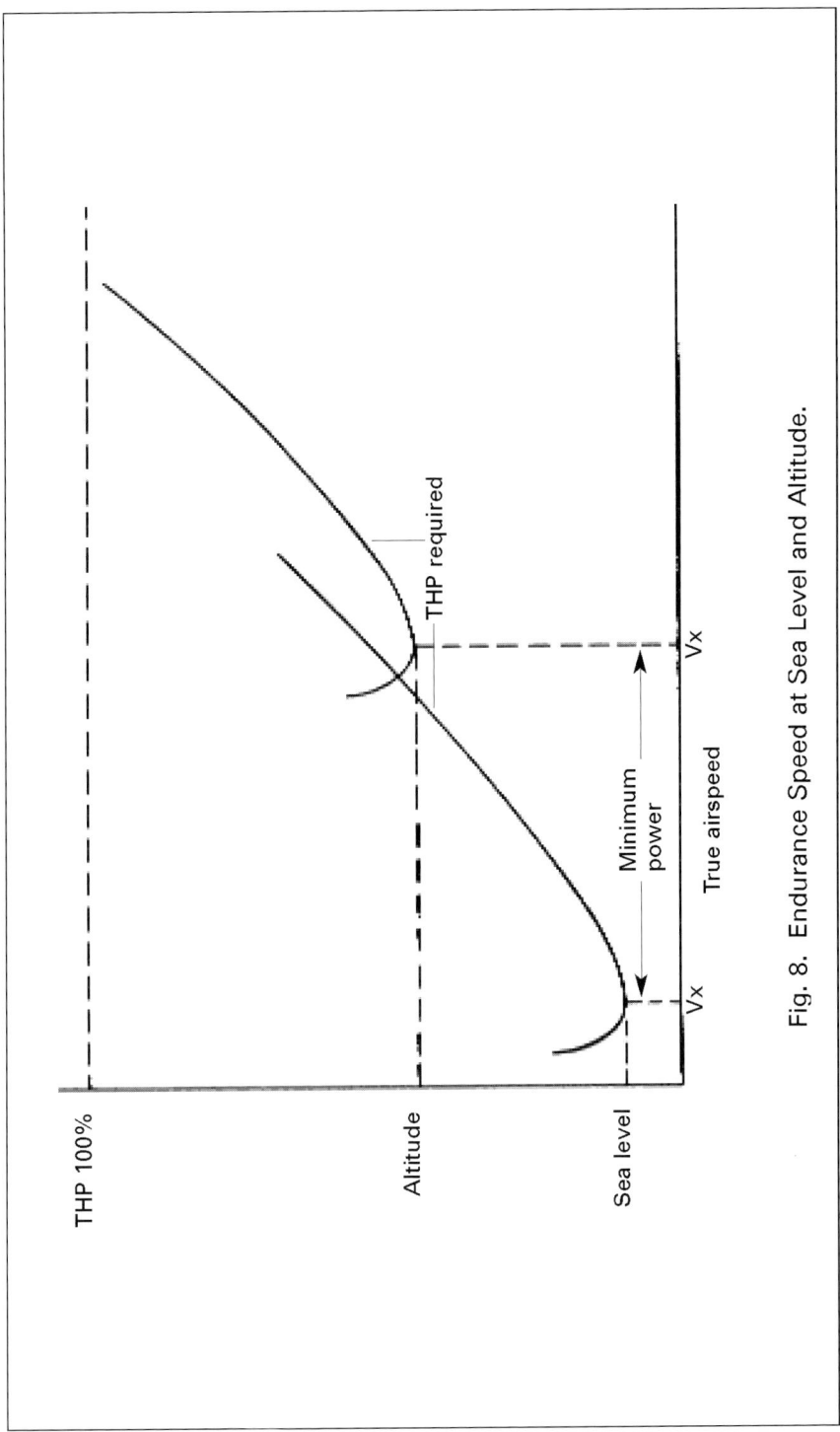

Fig. 8. Endurance Speed at Sea Level and Altitude.

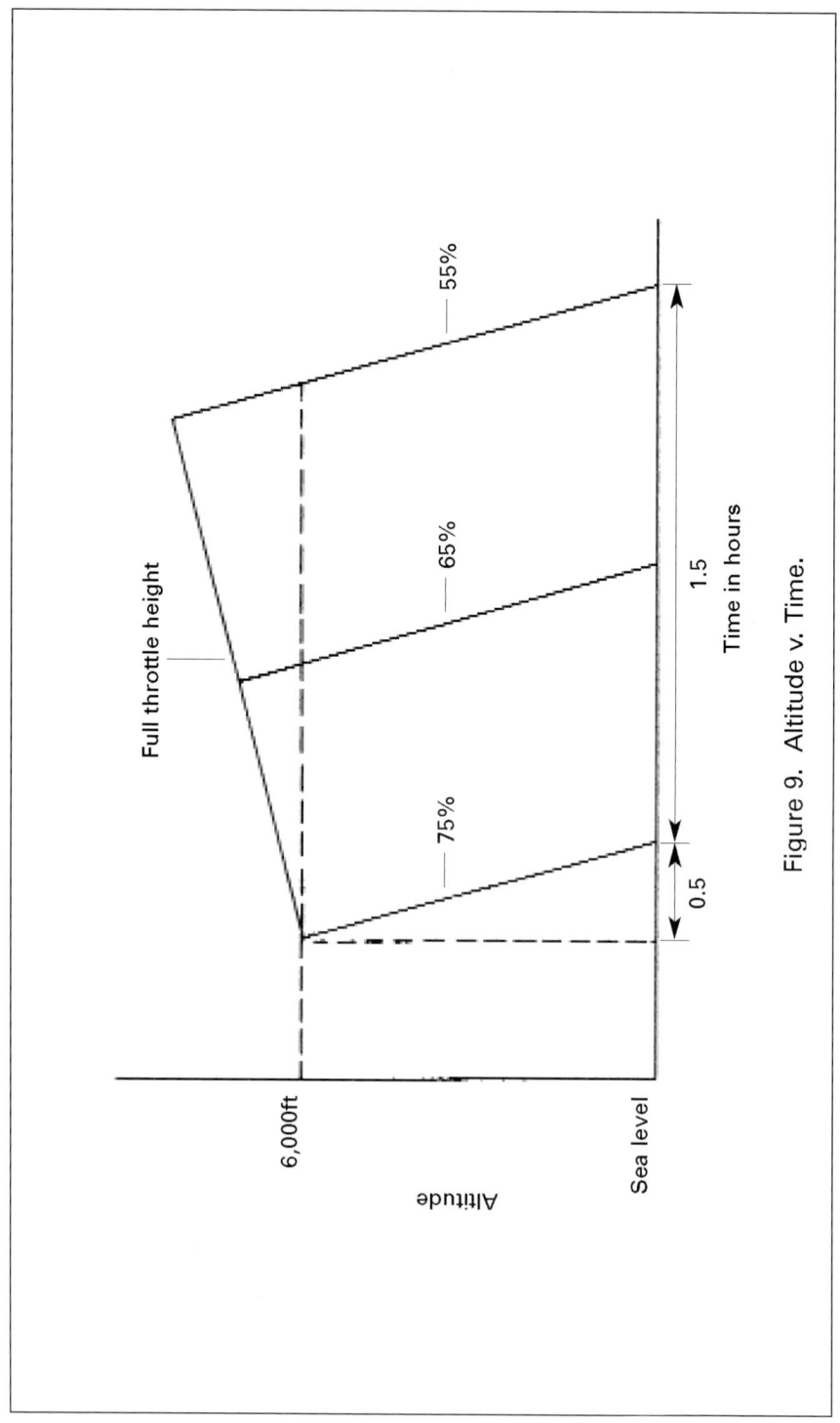

Figure 9. Altitude v. Time.

(range speed). The TAS is also lower, however, with the result that the product of drag multiplied by the TAS (power) is also lower. Therefore, less power and, more importantly, less fuel are used at the endurance speed than the minimum drag speed. It follows that if less fuel is used per unit of time, the endurance time will be extended. Flying lower and with less power will increase endurance, which is shown by Figure 9. Compare the endurance at 75 per cent brake horsepower with the endurance at 55 per cent brake horsepower; at the lower power setting, endurance is increased by 90min. It can also be seen that endurance is increased by 30min at any power setting by descending from 6,000ft to sea level. Nevertheless, the power setting has the greatest influence on endurance, altitude having a lesser effect, particularly for light aircraft with their low-power engines.

THE CLIMB

It is interesting to note that the maximum L/D ratio, or initial range speed, coincides with the maximum rate of climb speed (Vy), and that the endurance speed coincides with the maximum angle of climb speed (Vx). The last is approximately half-way between Vy and the flaps-up stalling speed (Vso), and is only used for obstacle clearance after take-off before reverting to Vy. During the cruise/climb, the rate of climb in feet per minute will be approximately half-way between the rates of climb achieved at Vx and Vy, but at a higher IAS.

Some pilots may argue that it is better to climb at the maximum rate of climb to cruise altitude, while others favour the cruise/climb method. Both techniques have their advantages.

Using the maximum rate of climb is advantageous where noise abatement procedures are called for, and it gives you more landing area options in the event of an engine failure on climb out. The cruise/climb method offers the benefits of better engine cooling, better visibility over the nose and a higher ground speed. It takes a minute or two longer to reach cruise altitude and burns just a couple of gallons more fuel. This is due to the fact that the engine is operating at climb power for that extra minute or two. Nevertheless, by the time the aircraft reaches the top of the climb, it is farther down the track. So as far as fuel efficiency and time are concerned, there's not much in it. Therefore, you may choose to start the initial climb at maximum rate before reverting to cruise/climb speed for the remainder of the ascent. (*See* also The Effects of Altitude and Weight earlier in this chapter.)

RANGE AND ENDURANCE DURING THE DESCENT

Three factors affect range and endurance during the descent: wind velocity, L/D ratio and the deficit thrust horsepower (DTHP). Where wind velocity is concerned, obviously flying into a headwind will reduce the ground speed and range, whereas a flying with a tailwind will have the opposite effect, just as in cruise flight.

The L/D ratio is explained by referring to Figure 10. The aerodynamic design of an aircraft dictates its L/D ratio – the greater the ratio, the flatter the glide angle. For example, gliders have very high lift/drag ratios when compared to powered aircraft, giving glide angles of up to 1 in 50 or so, compared with 1 in 12 or thereabouts for a basic light aircraft. Increasing the weight of an aircraft does not affect its L/D ratio. This is because the increased weight is balanced by increased lift, and the drag is balanced by an increase in thrust. Conversely, when gliding with the aircraft at a lower weight, less lift is required. It follows that since lift and drag are vectors of the aerodynamic total reaction produced by the wings, they are both reduced at lower weights. In trigonometric terms, the tangent of the glide angle is the same as the angle between the lift force and the total reaction. For the L/D ratio, the angle does not change. If the L/D ratio remains the same, so does the glide angle; therefore, the range on the glide remains the same whatever the weight.

Gliding at a lower weight can be accomplished at lower speed, but with the glide range remaining unchanged. This means that endurance on the glide is increased. The classic example is often shown in the movies, an aircraft suffering an engine failure, and the crew throwing out all the baggage and loose items. This would not stretch the glide, only prolong the time on the glide (endurance) by allowing a slower speed. If the speed is not reduced, nothing is gained by jettisoning the baggage!

Just as ETHP is the surplus power available for climbing and determines the rate of climb, DTHP determines the rate of sink during a power-off descent or glide. Remember that ETHP is the difference between THP available and THP required; THP available becomes less as power is reduced, and its curve moves down the graph until it meets the THP required curve. At this point, no ETHP is available for climbing and the aircraft will maintain straight-and-level flight. Reducing power further lowers THP available, and the curve moves farther down the graph, until at zero power, the graph's bottom line becomes the zero power line, indicating zero THP available. The difference between THP available (the bottom line) and THP required is now a negative value, known as deficit thrust horsepower (see Figure 6).

With an increase of altitude, the THP required curve moves up the graph and to the right, increasing the difference between THP required and THP available; thus, the DTHP increases. Therefore, the rate of descent at altitude is greater than at sea level. This is illustrated by the following formula:

$$\frac{DTHP \times 33,000}{Weight} = \text{rate of sink in feet per minute}$$

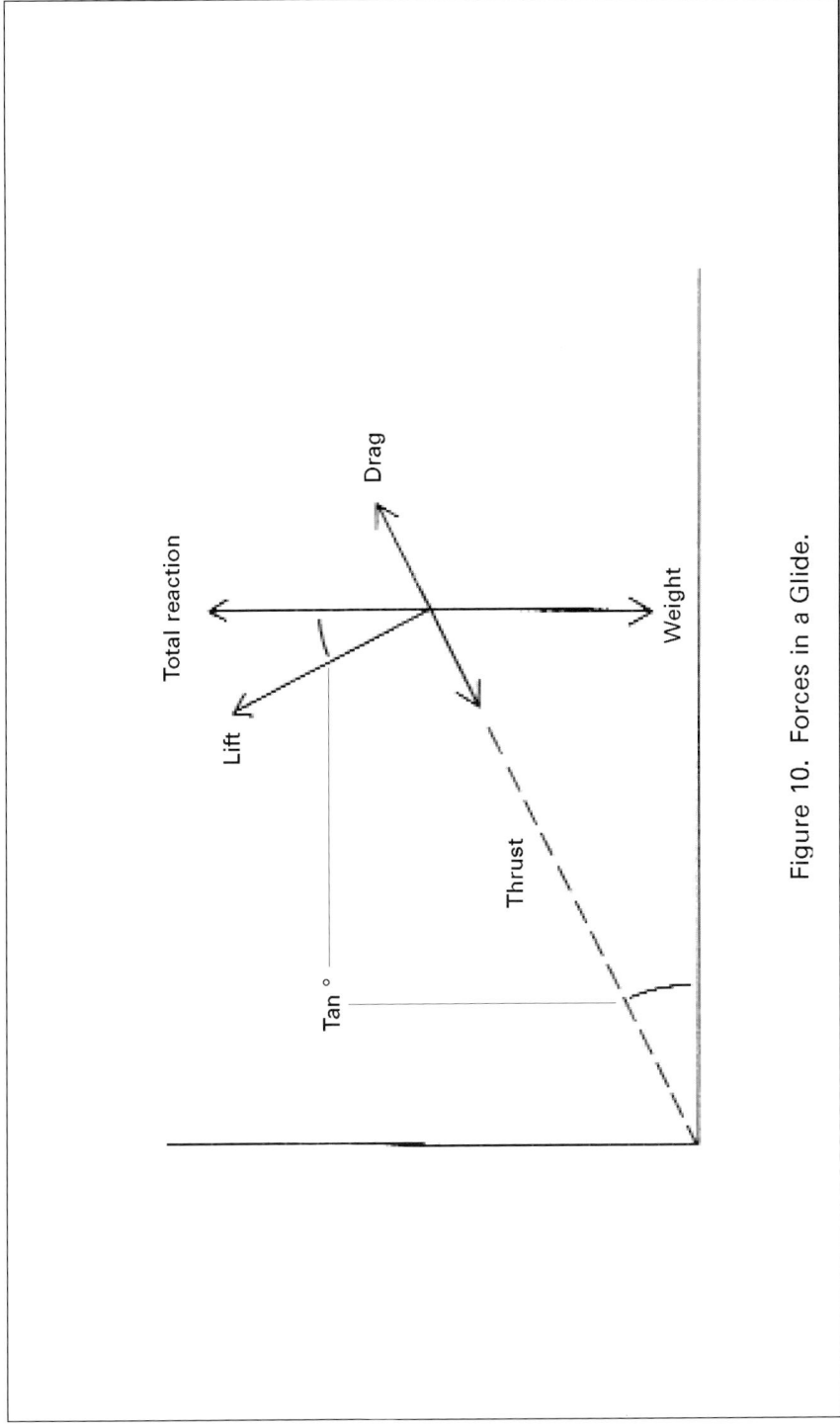

Figure 10. Forces in a Glide.

The Cessna Cardinal was introduced in 1967 with similar performance to the Cessna 172, having a range of 650–715n.miles (750–820st.miles) and a cruise speed of around 113kt (130mph). This is the fixed-gear version.

In Figure 6, it can be seen that DTHP at Vx at sea level is less than the Vy minimum power speed. Therefore, the minimum sink or lowest rate of descent will be less at Vx than at Vy, just as Vx produces a lower rate of climb than Vy. The maximum rate of climb speed (Vy) is also the same speed used for the maximum glide ratio with no power. This is the speed at which the aircraft will cover the greatest horizontal distance, or range, for height lost. The aircraft's POH should include a diagram showing the distance covered from given altitudes in still-air conditions. This should be approximately one mile per thousand feet of altitude descended at Vy. The rate of descent at Vy (best glide ratio) is about 15 per cent greater than at the minimum sink speed, Vx, due to minimum drag. (Remember that Vx is the speed for endurance flying.)

When descending at the minimum sink speed, the aircraft will not glide as far (reduced range). However, it will remain airborne for longer (greater endurance). In the event of an engine failure, using Vx will give you more time to search for a forced landing area, which you should have in mind already. Increasing speed to maximum glide ratio (Vy) will allow you to cover a greater distance on the descent, which could be a benefit if the wind is making your forced landing circuit difficult. The disadvantage of using Vx is that it is closer to the stalling speed, and you don't want to stall the aircraft while planning your descent route to a forced landing area, or during turns toward the field. Increase the airspeed by 10kt during the turns to allow a safety margin above the increased stalling speed. Stalling and spinning-in happen all too often in this situation. The glide angle suffers more from flying too slow than too fast, due to the increased drag on the back side of the power curve, that is at a speed below Vx.

For normal cross-country flying, it is more fuel efficient to employ the cruise descent method, in which altitude is lost gradually, within the constraints of ATC requirements, terrain clearance, etc. Ideally, the descent should be started at a distance from the destination that allows 5n.miles to be covered for every 1,000ft of altitude to be descended. The distance can be calculated by simply multiplying the altitude (minus the last three digits) by five. For example:

Altitude to be descended = 7,000ft
Distance at which descent to be started = 7 x 5 = 35n.miles.

Reducing engine power by 200–300rpm, or manifold pressure by 2–3in hg,

Mooney aircraft have always been noted for their high cruise speeds and economical operation. This Mooney 201 has a top speed of 175kt (200mph). With 242ltr (53imp.gal/64USgal) in the fuel tanks and a cruise speed of 160kt (184mph), it has a range of around 895n.miles (1,300st.miles) with an endurance of approximately 5hr 35min.

will produce the required rate of descent, which should be in accordance with the following table:

Ground speed (kt)	Rate of descent (ft/min)
90	300
120	400
150	500
180	600

Note: For every 30kt increase in ground speed, the rate of descent increases by 100ft/min.

Using the table as a guide, establish a suitable cruise descent ground speed and rate of descent for your aircraft. The same speed may be used during the cruise, or slightly higher. Increasing speed into the airspeed indicator's yellow arc should be done with caution to avoid overstressing the airframe if turbulence is encountered. Turbo-prop aircraft do not have a yellow arc on the airspeed indicator, so the red line is at the top of the green arc. This is a safety feature required by different certification standards that apply to transport aircraft.

Fuel flow during the descent is usually calculated at the normal cruise value, although it will be lower due to the reduced power setting used. The fuel saved will be a bonus above that planned. That said, in light aircraft, the saving does not amount to much, but in large transport aircraft it is significant. Planning the descent at the end of a cross-country flight is just as important as planning the cruise phase of the trip; aim to make a fuel-efficient and gradual descent to your destination airport. Ideally, the descent should take twice as long as the climb to ensure maximum fuel efficiency. It's more comfortable for the passengers too!

CONCLUSION

The price of aviation fuel rises constantly, dictated by the world's ever growing demand for oil based products – and fuel costs are one of the major expenses in operating an aircraft. If the amount of fuel consumed on each flight can be reduced, the operational cost of the aircraft can be cut substantially. This can be achieved by careful flight planning, correct engine handling and efficient fuel management, as described in this book.

You need a good technical knowledge of any aircraft you fly, and understanding the fuel system in its entirety forms an important part of that knowledge. Knowing where each part of the system is located and how it works, and having an understanding of the accuracy of the fuel gauges are imperative to ensure safe flight.

Fuel management involves refuelling the aircraft with the correct amount and type of fuel, and using the correct refuelling procedures. Just as important is the correct handling of fuel during flight. Knowing when to

The Beech 17 Staggerwing, with its radial engine and negative-stagger wings, was introduced in 1932 and is still a popular aircraft. A choice of engines from 330bhp upward produces a cruise speed of around 175kt (200mph) with a range of approximately 730n.miles (900st.miles). The cruise speed betters that of the much later 160kt (184mph) Beech V35 Bonanza.

change tanks, how to keep a record of fuel used and fuel remaining, and when to land for more fuel to safely continue your flight are all aspects of good airmanship.

Oil is just as important as fuel. Make sure the engine is supplied with the correct type and quantity of oil. Common sense airmanship is essential to alleviate any engine problems due to lack of fuel or oil that could compromise range and endurance.

Leaning the fuel/air mixture is one of the major methods of achieving lower fuel consumption. When doing so, however, it is most important to follow the engine manufacturer's instructions. These can be found in the POH or the aircraft's flight manual, or on placards attached to the instrument panel. The correct leaning procedure will ensure longer engine life, save fuel and money, and increase the range and endurance of the aircraft by as much as 20 per cent.

You should have an appreciation of the need and advantage of leaning the mixture, and the different methods available to achieve the correct fuel/air ratio. An understanding of the terms 'rich mixture', 'best power', 'best economy', 'maximum temperature' and 'stoichiometric settings' is essential

The Beech V35 Bonanza has been a very popular, high-performance and economical personal transport aircraft since its introduction in 1945. The high cruise speed of 160kt (184mph) and endurance of 4hr 45min give it a range of 765n.miles (880st.miles).

to achieve maximum range and endurance. Leaning should always be carried out with caution, though. Too lean a mixture can damage the engine; retarding the mixture control too far will cut off the fuel supply to the engine. This is the reason for the knurled shape of the mixture control and it red colour – for caution!

Carburettor or induction icing can starve your engine of the correct fuel/air mixture, causing a loss of power and bringing an end to your flight. Check for carburettor icing before take-off and frequently during flight by the judicious use of the carburettor heat control or anti-icing system, especially when ambient temperature is below 20°C (68°F) and relative humidity is greater than 60 per cent. A sound knowledge of carburettor icing and the different atmospheric conditions that induce it is essential. Do not become a victim of carburettor icing; it can severely reduce your aircraft's range and endurance.

Flight planning is a major subject in its own right, far greater than the brief description possible in this book. However, the information presented here in respect of planning for range and endurance should prove adequate for most pilots. It is imperative that you have a thorough understanding of the fuel required to cover each portion of a flight and the legal requirements pertaining to reserve fuel. The minimum legal reserve is a very basic minimum, and the prudent pilot will allow a more generous margin for any unexpected contingencies. A competent pilot should have an appreciation of the differences and advantages of various methods of cruise control, and be able to select the appropriate method for any given flight plan. A fuel log should always be part of the navigation log, allowing fuel required and fuel remaining to be monitored. Correct calculation of the fuel required should ensure a safe and fuel-efficient flight.

Regardless of whether you fly on local training flights, scenic flights or long-distance cross-country flights, flying for range and endurance is no less important. In these days of expensive fuel, obtaining the maximum range for a given quantity of fuel requires flying the aircraft as efficiently as possible. Having read this book and absorbed its advice, you should never experience any fuel management problems; you should have an understanding of all the requirements for achieving maximum range and endurance in your aircraft. Running the risk of ending a flight with too little fuel remaining in the tanks, or even landing short of your destination, should never occur. Every arrival should be made at the planned destination without having to worry about a lack of fuel.

Be fuel wise and fly safely!

Example C, Endurance

Given: Consumption = 75ltr/hr
        Total fuel = 275ltr

$$\frac{75\text{ltr/hr}}{60} \cdots \frac{275\text{ltr}}{03.40} = \text{answer}$$

Note: In this example, the answer is on the inner scale of the computer.

3. Still-Air Range and Endurance

The purpose of this formula is to find the still-air range (SAR) and endurance, given the total fuel, fuel flow and true airspeed (TAS). Set the total fuel on the inner scale, read off the SAR above the TAS, and endurance in minutes over the '60' index. With this method, we can find two answers in one setting on the computer.

Formula

$$\frac{\text{Total fuel}}{\text{Fuel flow}} \cdots \frac{\text{SAR}}{\text{TAS}} \cdots \frac{\text{Endurance}}{60} = \text{answer}$$

Example

Given: Total fuel = 390lb
        Fuel flow = 90lb/hr
        TAS = 175kt

$$\frac{390\text{lb}}{90\text{lb/hr}} \cdots \frac{758\text{n.miles}}{175\text{kt}} \cdots \frac{260\text{min}}{60} = \text{answer}$$

Therefore, the still-air range is 758n.miles, and endurance is 260min.

4. Elapsed Time Interval and Fuel Required

When flight planning a trip or during flight, the estimated time interval (ETI) and fuel required to cover a given distance can be found when the distance, ground speed (G/S) and fuel flow are known. These two problems can be solved in one setting on the computer.

Formula

$$\frac{\text{Distance}}{\text{G/S}} \cdots \frac{\text{ETI}}{60} \cdots \frac{\text{fuel required}}{\text{fuel flow}} = \text{answer}$$

Example

Given: Distance = 75n.miles
         Fuel flow = 85ltr/hr
         G/S = 145kt

$$\frac{75\text{n.miles}}{145\text{kt}} \quad \cdots \quad \frac{00.31}{60} \quad \cdots \quad \frac{44\text{ltr}}{85\text{ltr/hr}} = \underline{\text{answer}}$$

Therefore, to cover the given distance, the fuel required is 44ltr, while ETI is 31min.

5. Air and Ground Nautical Miles per Pound from Fuel Consumption

From known fuel consumption, true airspeed in knots (KTAS) and ground speed (G/S), air and ground nautical miles per pound of fuel can be found.

Formula

$$\frac{10}{\text{fuel consumption}} \quad \cdots \quad \frac{\text{anm/lb}}{\text{KTAS}} \quad \cdots \quad \frac{\text{gnm/lb}}{\text{G/S}} = \underline{\text{answer}}$$

Example

Given: Fuel consumption = 58lb/hr
         KTAS = 125kt
         G/S = 103kt

$$\frac{10}{58\text{lb/hr}} \quad \cdots \quad \frac{2.15\text{anm/lb}}{125\text{kt}} \quad \cdots \quad \frac{1.77\text{gnm/lb}}{103\text{kt}} = \underline{\text{answer}}$$

Therefore, the answers indicated on the outer scale are 2.15anm/lb and 1.77gnm/lb.

6. Ground Nautical Miles per Pound from Distance Flown and Fuel Used

Given the distance flown and the amount of fuel used, the ground nautical miles per pound can be found.

Formula

$$\frac{\text{Distance (n.miles)}}{\text{Fuel (lb)}} \quad \cdots \quad \frac{\text{gnm/lb}}{10} = \underline{\text{answer}}$$

Example

Given: Distance = 460n.miles
         Fuel = 360lb

$$\frac{460\text{n.miles}}{360\text{lb}} \quad \cdots \quad \frac{1.27\text{gnm/lb}}{10} = \underline{\text{answer}}$$

Therefore, the fuel consumption is 1.27gnm/lb.

7. Fuel Consumption in Air or Ground Nautical Miles per Pound

This formula is another alternate method of calculating air or ground nautical miles per pound of fuel.

Formula

$$\frac{\text{KTAS (or G/S)}}{\text{Fuel flow}} \quad \cdots \quad \frac{\text{anm/lb or gnm/lb}}{10} = \underline{\text{answer}}$$

Example

Given: KTAS or G/S = 125kt
         Fuel flow = 58lb/hr

$$\frac{125\text{kt}}{58\text{lb/hr}} \quad \cdots \quad \frac{2.15\text{anm/lb or gnm/lb}}{10} = \underline{\text{answer}}$$

Therefore, the fuel consumption is 2.15anm/lb or gnm/lb, depending on whether you use airspeed or ground speed.

GLOSSARY

All-up weight (AUW) The total weight of the aircraft at any given time.

Angle of attack (Alpha) The angle made between the chord line and the relative airflow.

Anti-knock rating A measure of a fuel's resistance to detonation.

Auxiliary pump A fuel pump that is not engine driven, usually being electrically powered. *See* also fuel pump.

Auxiliary tank A tank containing a reserve of fuel. *See* also reserve tank.

Bag tank A tank made from flexible material, such as rubber, and not part of the airframe.

Best economy A mixture setting for maximum fuel economy.

Bonding An earth return system to dissipate static electricity.

Brake horsepower A measure of the power developed by the engine.

Calorific value The amount of heat realized from the fuel, measured in Joules/kg.

Carbon dioxide (CO_2) A gas produced by combustion.

Cross-feed Feeding fuel to engine(s) from tank(s) on opposite side of aircraft, usually after an engine failure or to balance lateral trim.

Density ratio The ratio of air density at sea level to air density at altitude.

Detonation Uncontrolled combustion in a piston engine, caused by too low a fuel grade for the engine, too much compression or over-supercharging.

Dipping Measuring the fuel quantity with a marked stick.

Drag/velocity ratio The ratio of drag to velocity.

Drain cock *See* weather head.

Endurance speed The speed at which the least amount of fuel is used per unit of time.

Equi-time point The position on track from which it takes the same amount of time to reach the destination as to return to the departure point.

Evaporative icing Ice forming in the engine's induction system due to evaporative cooling.

Flash point The temperature at which the ignition of a flammable substance takes place.

Fractions Products (petrol, kerosene, diesel, etc) derived from crude oil during the refining process.

Fuel/air ratio The ratio of fuel to air in the mixture supplied to the engine by the carburettor.

Fuel capacity The actual volume of fuel in the tanks. Gauged fuel should be the same as the capacity when the tanks are full.

Fuel drain port A valve in the lowest part of a fuel tank to allow emptying.

Fuel exhaustion All fuel totally consumed.

Fuel inlet port A point near the bottom of a fuel tank from which fuel is piped to the engine.

Fuel pump A device for supplying fuel to the engine under positive pressure. Pumps may be driven by the engine or electrically. *See* also auxiliary pump.

Fuel starvation Fuel available prevented from flowing to the engine.

Fuel tank vent An orifice in the fuel tank that allows fumes to escape to atmosphere, and air to enter as fuel is drawn off, preventing a vacuum.

Full-throttle height The height above which engine power decreases with throttle wide open.

Gauged fuel The sum of fuel-gauge readings, including any unusable fuel.

Go-around An aborted landing.

Grounding clip A means of attaching an earthing wire near the fuel filler hole when refuelling.

Heptane An alkaline hydrocarbon; zero octane fuel reference.

Hydrocarbon A hydrogen and oxygen compound.

Ideal mixture *See* stoichiometric mixture.

Integral tanks Fuel tanks that form part of the aircraft's structure.

KTAS True airspeed in knots.

L/D ratio The ratio of lift to drag; a measure of a wing's efficiency.

Leaning Adjusting the fuel/air mixture to the desired setting.

Maximum all-up weight (MAUW) The total permissible weight of an aircraft, including all fuel, fluids, occupants and cargo. Also known as maximum gross weight. *See* also maximum take-off weight.

Maximum take-off weight (MTOW) The maximum weight at which an aircraft can safely take off.

Mineral oil Kerosene-based oil.

Octane rating A number indicating a fuel's position on the scale of resistance to detonation. Also anti-knock rating.

Optimum cruise speed The speed at which the least amount of fuel is used per unit of velocity.

Performance number Similar to octane rating, but greater than 100.

Pilot's operating handbook (POH) A manual provided by the aircraft manufacturer, containing essential information for the correct and safe operation of the aircraft.

Point of no return The position on track at which an aircraft does not have sufficient fuel to return to the point of departure.

Pre-ignition Fuel in a piston engine being ignited spontaneously before the spark plugs fire.

Ramp weight An aircraft's maximum allowable weight prior to taxiing.

Range speed The speed at which the least amount of fuel is consumed per unit of distance.

Relative humidity A percentage degree of saturation of a volume of atmosphere.

Reserve tank *See* auxiliary tank.

Specific air range (SAR) The distance flown for a given fuel consumption.

Selector A fuel flow valve.

Specific gravity The density of a liquid expressed as a fraction of water at 4°C (39°F).

Static electricity The build-up of an electrical charge, caused by the friction of air flowing over the aircraft, or by fuel flowing through a hose.

Sticking *See* dipping.

Stoichiometric mixture Fuel/air ratio in exact proportions for combustion.

Synthetic oil Man-made oil from chemicals.

TAS The true speed of the aircraft through the air.

Tetraethyl lead A product added to petrol to prevent detonation, producing leaded fuel.

Thermal efficiency The percentage ratio of work done to heat energy from fuel burned per unit of time.

Thrust horsepower (THP) The horsepower delivered by the propeller.

Thrust horsepower available The thrust available to propel the aircraft.

Thrust horsepower required The thrust required to propel the aircraft .

Tip tank A streamlined fuel tank located on the wing tip. *See* also auxiliary tank and reserve tank.

Throttle icing Ice in the carburettor, on or near the butterfly valve.

Undrainable fuel All fuel remaining in the tank and fuel lines after draining the tank.

Unusable fuel Fuel remaining in the bottom of the tank, below the level of the fuel inlet port.

Usable fuel Same as flight-plan fuel, but excluding reserve fuel.

Weather head A hand operated valve for draining fuel from a tank.

Vaporization Liquid, such as fuel, turning to gas.

V/D ratio The ratio of velocity to drag.

Volatile Fuel having a high vapour pressure.

Vso Stalling speed with flaps down.

Vx Best angle of climb speed.

Vy Best rate of climb speed.

BIBLIOGRAPHY

Van Sickle, N.D, *Modern Airmanship*, Van Reinhold, 1957.
Milne-Thomson, L.M., *Theoretical Aerodynamics*, Courier Dover Publications, 1973.
Stinton, D., *The Design of the Aeroplane*, Grenada Publications, 1983.
Kermode, A.C., *Mechanics of Flight*, Longman Scientific & Technical, 1987
Gunston, B., *Jane's Aerospace Dictionary*, Jane's Publishing, 1980.
Campbell, R.D., *Ground Training*, Vol. III, Collins Professional & Technical Books.
Pilot's Handbook of Aeronautical Knowledge, U.S. Department of Transportation.
Hames, C.S., *Commercial Pilot*, Technical Education Publications, 1965.
Wells, A.T., *Flight Safety, a Primer for General Aviation Pilots*, TAB Books/McGraw-Hill, 1992.
Smith, H., *The Illustrated Guide to Aerodynamics*, TAB Books/McGraw Hill, 1985.

Other Books by the Same Author
Propeller Aerodynamics, the History, Aerodynamics & Operation of Aircraft Propellers. Devoted entirely to aircraft propellers, and written with the private and commercial pilot in mind.
Petone to Pencarrow, A Shoreline with a History. A local history of Wellington, New Zealand's east harbour shoreline.

INDEX